THE OLYMPICS

FASTEST, HIGHEST,

LONGEST, STRONGEST

Written by

David Arscott

Created and designed by

David Salariya

SCRIBO

'Sport is a school of justice, democracy and human rights.'

Juan Antonio Samaranch

'The Olympics remain the most compelling search for excellence that exists in sport, and maybe in life itself.'

Dawn Fraser

'For too long the world has failed to recognise that the Olympic Games and the Olympic Movement are about fine athletics and fine art.'

Avery Brundage

'To anyone who has started out on a long campaign believing that the gold medal was destined for him, the feeling when all of a sudden the medal has gone somewhere else is quite indescribable.'

Seb Coe

'A lifetime of training for just ten seconds.'

Jesse Owens

Contents

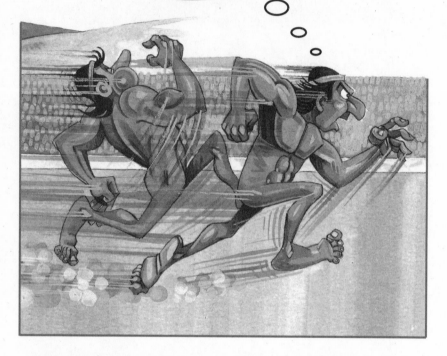

Coroebus suddenly remembered that he'd left a light under the onions.

GREEK

BEGINNINGS

I n 776 BC a cook named Coroebus sprinted across the finishing line at Elis in southern Greece and into the history books. He'd just become the earliest recorded Olympic champion.

If the Games had started even before that, as some historians think, they hadn't yet taken off. Our cook's 190-metre (210-yard) dash was the only event on the programme!

Over the centuries, however, the event was to blossom into a five-day extravaganza which attracted aspiring (and perspiring) athletes from well beyond Greece itself.

Mind you, there was a lot of competition across the so-called panhellenic world, with no fewer than four major tournaments on the go:

- **The Olympic Games**
The daddy of them all, held every four years at Elis in honour of the king of the gods, Zeus. The prize was an olive wreath.
- **The Pythian Games**
Also every four years, near Delphi and in honour of Apollo.
Prize: a laurel wreath.
- **The Isthmian Games**
Every two years, near Corinth, in honour of Poseidon.
Prize: a pine wreath.
- **The Nemean Games**
Every two years, near Nemea, in honour of Zeus. Prize: a wreath of wild celery. (Well, it was better than nothing, wasn't it?)

Although the Games began as a religious festival, they gradually turned into a rip-roaring public jamboree, culminating in a gigantic ox-roast barbecue.

The main stadium could seat 50,000 people, and the crowds who flocked into the valley at Elis were entertained by jugglers and acrobats, harangued by politicians and accosted by traders seeking a quick drachma.

SUPERHEROES

If you'll forgive a brief Greek lesson, the *gymnos* in the word *gymnasium* means 'naked'. Take a look at ancient vases, sculptures and mosaics and you'll see that the supremely fit athletes wooed their adoring crowds while performing completely in the buff.

And never mind the symbolic wreaths – although the winners received no cash prizes on the day itself, they were feted like the sports stars of today, having statues erected in their honour, receiving countless perks and finding themselves with a choice of rich women to marry. They'd arrived!

A FAREWELL TO ARMS

The Games were regarded as so important that there was a brief truce around the sanctuary (or Altis) every four years, with the athletes and their families being granted safe passage through the country. Was it honoured? Apparently so, because no walls were built around the site in early times. That would have been asking for big trouble anywhere else in battle-happy Greece. No weapons were allowed inside during the Games – and executions were put on hold.

MEN ONLY

It's disgraceful, of course, but women (along with slaves and foreigners) were barred from taking part. Worse still, married women weren't even allowed to watch – and faced the death penalty if they did. Here's what the writer Pausanias had to say: 'As you go from Scillus along the road to Olympia there is a mountain with high, precipitous cliffs. It is called Mount Typaeum. It is a law of Elis to cast down it any women who are caught present at the Olympic games.'

One thing they *could* do was enter a chariot in the arena, although they wouldn't be there to see it win. For the record, the first female Olympics champion of this kind (in 396 BC) was Kynisca, a sister of the king of Sparta, whose team won the four-horse chariot race. Perhaps it was some consolation that the women – although only unmarried ones – were allowed to take part in their own games, a series of running races called the Heraia.

CAUGHT IN THE ACT

In 404 BC a woman called Callipateira disguised herself as a trainer so that she could watch her son perform in the Games. Unfortunately for her, she suffered a bit of an embarrassment while climbing out of the trainers' enclosure. Her clothing slipped, revealing her little secret to the world at large.

It seems that the authorities spared her from the death penalty because of her family's oustanding athletic pedigree – but they imposed a new rule under which all trainers, like the athletes, must always appear naked.

GETTING FIT

The athletes took their training very seriously, with a dedication equal to anything we'd see in a 21st century gym. They were supposed to start preparing themselves months in advance and to turn up at what we'd today think of as the Olympic Village several weeks before the event began. For some of them this was at the end of an exhausting journey from places as far away as Spain, Egypt and the Black Sea.

As they went through their exercises their 'personal trainers' would use long sticks to point out any signs of an incorrect posture. The Greeks believed harmonious movement was just as important as physical strength. To make this easier they often employed flute players to aid their rhythm and tranquillity.

It could be a messy business:

- They first smeared themselves with olive oil.
- They then dusted themselves with fine sand to regulate their body temperature.
- They might then wrestle on squirmy clay.
- Finally they scraped off all the muck and sweat with a curved metal tool called a strigil.

Young Alexis got plenty of stick from his trainer.

The Greek philosopher Epictetus had this stern advice for anyone who wanted to win an Olympic prize: 'You will have to obey instructions, eat according to regulations, keep away from desserts, exercise on a fixed schedule at definite hours, in both heat and cold; you must not drink cold water nor can you have a drink of wine whenever you wish. You must hand yourself over to your coach exactly as you would to a doctor.'

ENTER A WIMP

The author Lucian, born around AD 125, gives us a good idea of the training regime in his day. He invents a dialogue between the statesman Solon and the philosopher Anacharsis – a foreigner who has never been to the Games and can't understand why all these young men are exhausting themselves in the gymnasium and sometimes getting hurt in the process. (Today he'd say football was 22 grown men chasing a piece of leather.)

'It won't be easy to convince me,' he says, 'that people who behave like this aren't wrong in the head.'

Where he comes from, he adds, 'we wouldn't take a single box around the ears – we're such cowards'.

Solon explains how tough the regime is: 'We accustom them to running, both long distance and sprinting. And they have to run not on hard ground with a good footing, but in deep sand on which you can neither tread firmly nor get a good push-off, the foot sinking in.

'Then, to fit them to leap a trench or other obstacle, we make them practise with leaden dumb-bells in the hands. And, again, there are distance matches with the javelin . . .'

His visitor, he says, would delight in 'looking at the men's courage and physical beauty'. (The Greeks did like a well-toned body.)

And here are a few of his arguments in favour of Olympic training:

- It hardened the body.
- It increased endurance.
- It improved health.
- It taught courage, and so prepared young men for battle.

MODERN OLYMPIC VENUES

1896	Athens, Greece
1900	Paris, France
1904	St. Louis, United States
1906	Athens, Greece [unofficial]
1908	London, United Kingdom
1912	Stockholm, Sweden
1920	Antwerp, Belgium
1924	Paris, France
1928	Amsterdam, Netherlands
1932	Los Angeles, United States
1936	Berlin, Germany
1948	London, United Kingdom
1952	Helsinki, Finland
1956	Melbourne, Australia
1960	Rome, Italy
1964	Tokyo, Japan
1968	Mexico City, Mexico
1972	Munich, West Germany
1976	Montreal, Canada
1980	Moscow, USSR
1984	Los Angeles, United States
1988	Seoul, South Korea
1992	Barcelona, Spain
1996	Atlanta, United States
2000	Sydney, Australia
2004	Athens, Greece
2008	Beijing, China
2012	London, United Kingdom
2016	Rio de Janeiro, Brazil
2020	Tokyo, Japan

THE EVENTS

As in the modern Olympics, events were added to (and dropped from) the programme over time. Here's the pick of the bunch:

Pentathlon
As the name implies, this comprised five different sports – the long jump, javelin, discus, a sprint and wrestling. It was regarded as the toughest event of them all, and was used by the military to prepare young soldiers for the battlefield.

The philosopher Aristotle recognised another benefit. The pentathlon, he observed, demanded a body attuned to the demands both of speed on the track and physical strength: 'This is why the athletes in the pentathlon are the most beautiful.' Hmm.

Running
The *stadion* was the original Olympic sprint event (about 200 yds / 180 m) and was later included in the pentathlon. The *diaulos* was a longer run of between 384 m (410 yds) and 768 m (840 yds), while the *dolichos* seems to

The Hoplites put up a real fight for first place

have varied over time between 1400 m (1540 yds) and 4 km (4,375 yds).

Hoplitodromos

The weirdest race of them all involved the runners shelving the no-clothes rule and running the length of the diaulos race in full hoplite uniform. This must have been great for army training, but since it's reckoned that the helmet, shield and greaves weighed at least 50 lbs (23 kg), you'd have needed quite a long rest between finishing a race and taking on the enemy.

Long jump

The athletes jumped into a bed of sand, as today, but from 70 BC they were allowed to use lead weights called 'halteres' in each hand to give themselves extra momentum. These were made from stone, lead or bronze, and from the evidence found at archaeological sites it seems that they were designed to suit the individual – they varied from around 1.6 kg (3½ lb) to 4.6 kg (10 lb). The athlete would swing them out in front on take-off and let them go once he was launched into the air. Because the Greeks placed so much emphasis on physical grace, it wasn't enough simply to jump further than anyone else. You had to land without toppling over or you'd be disqualified.

Discus

As with the halteres, it seems that the athletes were able to choose the size and weight of their discus to suit themselves. There were, otherwise, strict rules governing the sport.

The throwers stood inside a *balbis*, or throwing cage, and would be disqualified if they stepped outside the lines that surrounded it. And there was none of today's whirling around – they could swing the discus, but they were permitted to take only a single step forward before hurling it on its way.

But what style! Ancient vase-painters couldn't have done without them. It was the done thing for the winner to have his discus inscribed and dedicated to a god. One found at Olympia bears the message *'Kleon threw me to win the wreath'*.

AN ANCIENT WONDER

The pride of the sanctuary at Olympia was a statue of Zeus so glorious that it was regarded as one of the Seven Wonders of the World.

Designed by the renowned sculptor Phidias, it was all of 40 ft (12 m) tall and fashioned from gold and ivory. Zeus sat on a cedar throne studded with precious jewels, holding a statuette of the goddess of victory, Nike.

The Zeus figure presided over the temple from around 440 BC to AD 400, when – the Games now abandoned – it was removed to Constantinople (today's Istanbul). In AD 462 its new home burned down and it vanished for ever.

Javelin

There was a leather strap around the javelin's shaft, with holes for the athlete's middle and index fingers. This gave him a better grip, and therefore greater accuracy, but because the strap was placed at the centre of gravity, the throwing distance was increased, too. Apart from the straightforward javelin event as part of the pentathlon, there was a separate competition for accuracy. For this the athletes would throw at a target while riding a horse.

TAKE YOUR SEAT AT THE GAMES

From the 77th Olympiad in 472 BC the games were stretched out over five days. Here's a typical programme:

Day 1 – First the athletes and the judges (the hellanodikai) take the Olympic oath in front of the great statue of Zeus. A competition is held for heralds and trumpeters, the winners earning the right to proclaim the Olympic victors throughout the week. Next the competitors visit the sacred olive grove, the Altis, and pray for victory. Then everyone journeys to the stadium for the grand opening ceremony. The only sports held on the first day are the running, wrestling and boxing events for boys.

Day 2 – The main event begins in the hippodrome, with a grand procession followed by various horse and chariot events. In the afternoon the action switches to the stadium, where the pentathlon is held. The day ends with a ritual at the shrine of Pelops, Zeus's grandson, so underlining the religious inspiration of the Games.

Day 3 – The morning is taken up with a huge festive procession by priests, athletes, judges and representatives of all the Greek cities, with the sacrifice of a hundred oxen in honour of Zeus. The foot races are held in the afternoon, after which (of course) another banquet is held.

Day 4 – Now the 'heavy' events get under way – beginning with wrestling. Boxing comes next, followed by pankration (no-holds-barred wrestling) and, last of all, the foot race in full armour.

Day 5 – The day for the prize-giving, in front of Zeus's statue. A local lad has been chosen to cut a leafy branch from the ancient wild olive tree sacred to Zeus. Huge crowds look on as the victory wreaths are placed on a table of ivory and gold. The winning athletes come forward to be crowned, and then the feasting begins all over again – to continue until the early hours of the following morning.

Boxing
Although the athletes wore a rudimentary kind of glove (soft ox-leather strapped around the hands), this seems to have been for their own protection rather than to spare the face and body of their opponents. There were no weight limits, and a fight stopped only when one of the combatants was unable to carry on.

Greek writings and pictures on vases and tomb reliefs make it clear that broken noses and cauliflower ears were commonplace in what must have been a horrific sport.

Here's the satirist Lucillius, writing in the second century BC: 'When Odysseus returned safely to his home after twenty years, only his dog Argos recognised him. But neither dogs nor your fellow citizens can recognise you, Stratophon, after you have boxed for four hours.'

And what if one of the combatants died? Olympic rules gave athletes immunity if they killed an opponent, but a boxer named Kleomedes apparently took brutality to a new pitch. The judges refused to grant him an olive wreath after he bludgeoned his adversary to death – because they believed that he'd meant to do it.

Wrestling

Size mattered here, too. Although men were separated from boys, there were no weight divisions. The great wrestler Milo is said to have prepared for his bouts by eating 40 lbs of meat and bread in one go, washed down by two gallons (9 litres) of wine. He's also said to have carried a calf on his shoulders

THE OLYMPIC LAUREATE

The lyric poet Pindar, who produced a massive range of work during his long life (c.518–438 BC), made a good income from the Olympics and the three other panhellenic games. He toured Greece writing victory odes for the aristocratic champions, and no fewer than 44 of them have survived. The odes typically set the winner's glory in the context of his illustrious ancestors, throwing in myths of the Greek gods and heroes for good measure.

Pindar also wrote about the fate of the losers – telling how they would abjectly slink back to their home cities in disgrace.

every day in order to increase his stamina. True or not, he was obviously a man who demanded some respect. There were strict rules in wrestling. You weren't allowed to bite an opponent or grab him by the genitals, but broken bones were part of the risk you took. In '*orthia*' (upright) wrestling the object was to throw your opponent to the ground, and the first man to achieve this three times was the winner. This might take a long time, and the match continued non-stop until there was a result.

'*Kato*' (ground) wrestling went on until one of the athletes gave up. Defeat was indicated by raising the right hand with the index finger pointed – assuming, of course, that the joints were still in place.

Pankration
Here's the most ruthless Olympic sport you can imagine – a combination of boxing and wrestling which banned only biting and eye-gouging. That left punching, kicking, choking, finger-breaking, blows to the genitals and any other ploy an athlete could devise. Holding an opponent with one hand while

smashing him with another was safely within the rules, and it's not surprising to learn that serious injuries were commonplace and death an occasional inevitability. In one version of the game the loser was the man who hit the ground first. In another it was whoever first lost consciousness.

NAKED AGGRESSION

The legendary pankratist Dioxippus was crowned Olympic champion by default in 336 BC because no opponent could be found brave enough to face him. His most famous victory was achieved outside the ring. At a banquet organised by Alexander the Great, Dioxippus was challenged to a fight by a Macedonian soldier named Coragus.

The odds seemed stacked against him, because he fought naked with only a club for a weapon, whereas Coragus was fully armed, with a javelin, spear and sword.

You've guessed it! Dioxippus won the fight — confirming the high status of pankration.

Equestrian events

Although German archaeologists have been excavating the site of Olympia since 1875, it wasn't until as recently as 2008 that they at last found the site of the hippodrome, to the south-east of the sanctuary.

The bad news is that none of it is visible, because it was submerged under deep flood waters long ago. We do have a pretty good idea of its size, though: 1052 x 64m (1150 x 70 yards) inside the earth banks thrown up for the spectators.

The four-horse chariot race was first held at the Olympics in 680 BC, but the hippodrome programme kept on expanding with new additions:

- 648 BC Horse racing.
- 500 BC Apene races – two mules pulling a chariot.
- 496 BC Horse racing for mares.
- 408 BC Two-horse chariot race.
- 384 BC Chariot race with four colts.
- 268 BC Two-colt chariot races.
- 256 BC Horse racing for colts.

The charioteers weren't expected to perform naked like the athletes, which must have been something of a relief during a rough ride. On the other hand, although they must have been stars in their own right and were well rewarded, they didn't pick up any olive wreaths for their triumphs. Only the wealthiest families could afford to finance the sport, and these gilded aristocrats therefore picked up the prizes.

It was a dangerous business. Pindar recorded a race which began with 40 chariots and ended with only one.

DIRTY TRICKS

Winning an Olympic event gave an athlete such incredible status that it's not surprising to come across occasional evidence of skulduggery.

In 488 BC Gelo of Gala, a formidable soldier, won the chariot race and couldn't help but be impressed by Astylus of Croton, who picked up two wreaths in the running race. Soon afterwards Gelo became tyrant of Syracuse,

SPARTAN TREATMENT

In 420 BC, just after the start of the Peloponnesian War (Athens v Sparta, to keep it simple), the Spartans were handed the ultimate insult – being excluded from the Olympic games as a punishment.

That was too much for a Spartan named Lichas, who was desperate to win the chariot race. He pretended that his team came from Thebes – but when it won he ran onto the course in triumph, and so gave the game away.

A big mistake: the judges not only disqualified him, but instructed attendants to give him a public flogging.

and he persuaded Astylus to run for that city instead of his own – presumably with the help of a substantial bribe. This so infuriated the people of Croton that they tore down Astylus's Olympic statue and seized his house.

In 388 BC the judges established a new form of punishment, which was intended to hurt the pride and ruin the reputation of cheating athletes. A boxer named Eupolus had bribed no fewer than three opponents so that he could take the prize. When this came to light all four men were fined, and the money paid for a row of bronze statues of Zeus called 'zanes', each one inscribed with details of the men's foul play.

When Callipus of Athens was similarly found guilty of bribery in 332 BC his city sent an orator to Elis in the hope that he could induce the authorities to remit the fine. He couldn't, and so the Athenians decided to withdraw from the Games in protest. Apparently it was an utterance from the Oracle at Delphi (the words of the god Apollo transmitted by a priestess) which eventually persuaded them to change their minds – and soon another group of zane statues lined the roadside.

Even the revered judges could sometimes fall to temptation. In 396 BC three of them had to decide a neck-and-neck finish in a running race. Two came down for their local man, Eupolemus, while the third gave the verdict to Leon of Ambracia. When Leon appealed to the Olympic Council the two partisan judges were fined although, very strangely, Eupolemus was still declared the winner.

FROM NERO TO ZERO

The Roman emperor Nero was the most blatant cheat of them all. In AD67 he entered the chariot race, fell out of his cart and was almost crushed under the flying hooves – and yet was swiftly declared the winner.

It's hard to blame the judges. A man who'd killed his own mother would hardly accept public humiliation with a resigned shrug of the shoulders.

If you've kept an eye on the dates you'll realise that AD67 shouldn't have been an Olympic year at all, but Nero 'persuaded' the organisers of all four panhellenic games to stage their events one after the other while he was on a grand tour of his Greek possessions. He fancied himself as an artist, so he introduced singing events to the Olympics. (Yes, of course he won those, too.)

By this time the Games had lost their initial character. The Romans, who'd conquered Greece in 146 BC, preferred a dramatic show to athletic purity. Hot baths and other facilities were introduced, but the Olympics now favoured hardened professionals who knew how to put on a good show – even to the extent of boxers putting iron in their gloves to give the customers a bloody spectacle.

A series of earthquakes badly damaged the sanctuary at Elis during the third century AD, and barbarian attacks in AD 267 knocked it about a bit more, but the Romans had already desecrated it – robbing the treasury and converting the temple dedicated to the goddess Rhea into a shrine to 'the divine Augustus'.

REDISCOVERING OLYMPIA

The site of the original Olympic Games was lost for many centuries, thanks to a dire sequence of events reminiscent of the Biblical plagues.

- AD 426 – The emperor Theodosius II ordered the demolition of the temple of Zeus.
- AD 475 – The River Kladeos flooded, submerging the site beneath 5 m of water.
- AD 580 – The worst of a series of earthquakes demolished what remained.

When French excavations began in 1829, the site was submerged under metres of silt, thanks to continual flooding over the centuries. Extensive digs by German archaeologists followed, from 1875 into the modern period. Among the prized objects they found was a statue of Hermes, the messenger of the gods, by the great sculptor Praxiteles.

During the 1950s they located the workshop of Phidias, who created the huge statue of Zeus (**page 21**), finding sculptors' tools, terracotta moulds and a cup with the inscription 'I belong to Pheidias'.

There's now a modern museum on the site, telling the Olympic story and displaying a large collection of recovered artefacts, including notable bronzes, terracottas and mosaics.

The death knell sounded when the Christian emperor Theodosius the Great began a severe crackdown on pagan practices, banning sacrifices and forbidding people to visit sanctuaries, walk through temples or even gaze with admiration at classical statues.

In AD 393 he took this zealotry to the limit and banned the Olympic Games. After an almost incredible twelve centuries of largely noble endeavour, they now fell into a deep slumber for a further fifteen hundred years.

This fairy tale has a happy ending, with our Sleeping Beauty at last awoken from her long sleep – not by a handsome prince but by a young French aristocrat who took his inspiration from the regime of cold baths and physical exercise in English public schools.

ANCIENT OLYMPIC GREATS

The names of several early champions have been passed down to us.

Chonis (from Laconia) He was a running champion seven times, winning prizes in four consecutive Olympics (668–656 BC).

Gorgos (Elis) He won the pentathlon four times, and also triumphed in the diaulos and hoplitodromos events.

Hipposthenes (Sparta) A five-times wrestling champion.

Leonidas (Rhodes) He established the record of picking up no fewer than 12 olive wreaths in four consecutive Games (164–152 BC), winning the stadion, diaulos and hoplitodromos events in every one.

Milo (Croton) A wrestler who performed in seven Olympics and won six of them.

And spare a thought for the outstanding Arcadian wrestler **Arrachion**. He won the gruelling pankration competition three times, but knew nothing about his last victory in 564 BC – because he'd been throttled to death a split second before the judges accepted his opponent's submission and awarded him the verdict.

COUBERTIN'S DREAM

The American James Connolly became the first Olympic champion in 1,527 years when, with two hops and a jump, he won what we'd today call the triple jump in Athens on April 6th, 1896. He was presented with an olive branch, a silver medal (no gold then) and a diploma.

A mere 214 competitors from 14 countries took part in those first modern Olympic Games, and Connolly's later account of his experiences sums up the gloriously amateurish and somewhat ramshackle nature of the event.

To begin with he'd had to walk out of Harvard University, where he was an undergraduate, because the chairman of its athletics committee refused to give him an eight-week leave of absence for the Games. (Connolly would later be offered an honorary doctorate and would turn it down.)

There then followed a long, self-financed journey by boat and rail which almost ended in disaster. In Naples, after having his wallet stolen and with his train about to leave, Connolly had to tear himself away from policemen who wanted him to press charges against the thief. He rushed along the station platform, to be hauled through the window of the moving carriage by his fellow American athletes. 'If I had missed that train,' he wrote, 'I would not have reached Athens in time for my event.'

Immediately after his victory, 'a man in the front row of the stadium bowl waved his program at me. A woman beside him waved her gloved hand – a white glove. I waved back at them. Later I was told that they were the king and queen of Greece.

'At the tunnel entrance I was grabbed by a half-dozen bearded Greeks. One after the other they kissed me on both cheeks – guys I had never seen before – and their whiskers were oily. Five men – one of them left-handed – poised their pencils above their sketch pads, and one shouted, "Attonday, seel voo play!" And I attondayed until they all had done with sketching pictures of me.'

DR ARNOLD'S MEDICINE

The man behind this earnest, ambitious and sometimes undeniably comical revival of the Olympic spirit was Pierre de Frédy, Baron de Coubertin, who was born in Paris on the first day of 1863.

Coubertin was an intellectual who had rejected careers in the army and politics in order to promote educational reform. He was much taken by English public schools such as Rugby, whose former headmaster Dr Thomas Arnold had shown that sport could play a vital role in shaping a young man's character (yes, it was very much a man's world then) delivering 'moral and social strength'.

THE OTHER OLYMPIC GAMES

Hats off to Pierre de Coubertin, but a few other people got there first.

- In 1612 the English lawyer Robert Dover devised his so-called Olimpick Games at the Cotswold town of Chipping Campden. It's still held every Whitsun today, and includes some weird country sports such as shin-kicking, throwing the sledgehammer and duelling with willow sticks.

- Between 1796 and 1798, shortly after the French Revolution, a national 'Olympic Festival' included several track and field events from ancient times.

- In 1856 a wealthy Greek businessman, Evangelis Zappas, wrote to his king offering to finance an Olympics revival. It didn't quite come to that, but competitions between athletes from Greece and the Ottoman Empire were held in 1859, 1870 and 1875.

- In 1850 an English doctor, William Penny Brookes, founded the 'Olympian Games' in his home town of Much Wenlock, Shropshire. Designed 'to promote the moral, physical and intellectual improvement of the inhabitants', the event mixed athletics with traditional country sports such as quoits, cricket and football – and, like the Chipping Campden event, it's still held every year.

He went so far as to suggest that France had been defeated in the Franco-Prussian War (1870–71) because there wasn't enough physical exercise in its schools.

The French authorities weren't too excited by this pro-British enthusiasm (plenty of English public schoolboys would have agreed with them), but Coubertin, undaunted, founded the Union des Sociétés Françaises de Sports Athlétiques (USFSA) to spread his message.

'Let us export our oarsmen, our runners, our fencers into other lands,' he declared. 'That is the true Free Trade of the future.'

Reviving the Olympics was the obvious next step. After all, hadn't the ancient Greeks similarly been mad about mixing mental, moral and physical education to create the ideally rounded human being? Coubertin wasn't the first to have the idea of reviving the Games (*see facing page*), but he had the drive, contacts and influence to make it happen.

In 1892 he called a meeting of the USFSA in Paris, decked out the auditorium with neoclassical murals and other inspiring Greek devices and persuaded 79 delegates from nine countries to create the International Olympic Committee (IOC) which would organise the first modern Games.

FROM THE HORSE'S MOUTH

Here are a few more Coubertin *bons mots*:

• 'The important thing in life is not victory but combat; it is not to have vanquished but to have fought well.'

• 'For each individual, sport is a possible source for inner improvement.'

• 'All sports for all people.'

He borrowed a Latin phrase for the Olympic Motto – 'Swifter, higher, stronger!' – and also invented the Olympic Oath, which was first taken by the Belgian fencer Victor Boin during the 1920 event: 'In the name of all competitors I promise that we shall take part in these Olympic Games respecting and abiding by the rules that govern them, in the true spirit of sportsmanship, for the glory of sport and the honour of our teams.'

Victor let out a very loud Olympic oath

The original IOC rules stipulated that the presidency belonged to the country next hosting the games, which is why the businessman and author Demetrios Vikelas found himself in that unlikely position leading up to the 1896 event.

Unlikely? Well, he wasn't particularly interested in sport, but he happened to be living in Paris when Coubertin called the all-important meeting and was asked to turn up as a representative of Greece.

IOC PRESIDENTS

1894–1896	Demetrios Vikelas (Greece)
1896–1925	Baron Pierre de Coubertin (France)
1925–1942	Henri de Baillet-Latour (Belgium)
1946–1952	Sigrid Edström (Sweden)
1952–1972	Avery Brundage (USA)
1972–1980	Lord Killanin of Dublin and Spittal (Ireland)
1980–2001	Juan Antonio Samaranch (Spain)
2001–2013	Jacques Rogge (Belgium)
2013–	Thomas Bach (Germany)

He did a great job for his country: the original idea had been to hold the inaugural modern Olympics in Paris, but Vikelas persuaded the delegates that Greece was the obvious place to start. The Games had come home.

SLOW OUT OF THE BLOCKS

Although the 1896 event was regarded as a great success (the crowds in the Panathinaiko Stadium were said to be the largest ever to watch an international sporting contest), it took a while for the Olympic idea to catch fire.

To start with there was a wrangle over the next venue, in 1900. King George of Greece was keen for his country to host the Games on a permanent basis, and some of the first American competitors agreed with him.

Unfortunately for them, Paris had already been awarded this honour, which it proceeded to tarnish by integrating it with a World's Fair and dragging it out for all of five months. To this day it isn't clear which events were officially regarded as belonging to the Olympics and which were a mere sideshow.

The Paris Games had attracted roughly four times as many athletes as the Athens event, but numbers fell sharply in 1904, chiefly because it was held in the United States (at St Louis, Missouri) so demanding a long transatlantic boat journey for the European entrants. Coubertin himself didn't turn up.

These Olympics were once again attached to a World's Fair and they were once again extended over a lengthy period, but at least most of the events were designated as Olympic in nature – including some quaintly set aside specifically for schoolboys and Irish-Americans.

Athens did get another bite of the cherry in 1906, hosting the so-called Intercalated (or interleaved) Games, and the idea was the city would hold them at four-year intervals to nip and tuck with the major Olympics.

Although some 900 athletes turned up, these plans came to nothing. Some historians still steadfastly record the names of the winners, but the IOC doggedly regards these events as unofficial.

The Games at last became truly international in the two olympiads before the first world war. In 1908 (London) there were 2,000 competitors from 22 nations, and by 1912 (Stockholm) these figures had swollen further to 2,500 and 28 respectively. Pierre de Coubertin, elected IOC president in 1896 and (thanks to a change in the rules) destined to remain in the post until 1925, had seen his dream become a staggeringly successful reality.

OLYMPIADS

The 1896 Olympics were officially known as the Games of the I Olympiad, an olympiad being the four-year period (beginning on January 1) between each event.

All subsequent Games have followed this system, taking their number from the olympiad rather than the order in which they were held — so that the 1920 Antwerp Olympics (VII) followed the 1912 Stockholm Olympics (V), since there were no Games during the VI olympiad because of the First World War.

Mathematical head-scratchers will be pleased to learn that the Winter Olympics have always followed the normal numbering system.

THEY DID THINGS DIFFERENTLY THEN

If those early Games already had in them the seeds of today's fiercely competitive, lavishly financed, internationally rancorous, media-hyped extravaganza, they nevertheless often appear engagingly rough-edged and innocent to our eyes.

Here are a few things that simply wouldn't happen in a modern Olympics.

Anyone for tennis?
It wasn't necessary to qualify in advance for the 1896 Games, and some people took part simply because they were on holiday in Greece at the time. One of these was the Irishman John Boland. He put his name down for the tennis championships – and found himself winning both the singles and, with the German Friedrich Traun, the doubles too.

Troubled waters
Forget heated baths neatly divided into lanes – the 1896 swimming events were held in the Mediterranean Sea near Piraeus, and the

water was both choppy and distinctly chilly. The American swimmer Gardner Williams, who had travelled 5,000 miles to take part, jumped into the water to start his race – and then straight out again, defeated by the cold.

For the 1,200 metres freestyle race small boats ferried the contestants out to sea and abandoned them to cope with waves 12 ft (3.6 m) high. The course had been marked by lines of hollowed-out pumpkins, but these were now impossible to follow.

By the time Alfred Hajos from Hungary touched dry land to win, many of his rivals had had to be rescued from the water suffering from fatigue and numbness.

'My will to live completely overcame my desire to win,' Hajos said afterwards.

In Seine behaviour
The arrival of synchronised swimming as an Olympic event in 1984 makes it difficult for a modern observer to smile at earlier sports which failed to stand the test of time. Surely the strangest, though, was the swimming

obstacle race in the River Seine during the Paris Games of 1900. Competitors had to climb a pole, scramble over one line of boats and dive under another.

These Olympics included several odd features. The swimming races also took place in the Seine (*with* the current, which meant that times were very fast); long jumpers had to dig their own pits in the Bois de Boulogne because the facilities were so poor; and in the 400-metre hurdles the athletes had to jump over 30 ft (9.1 m) telephone poles.

Every bit as strange, though perhaps typically French, were the prizes – not medals, but *objets d'art* carefully graded by value.

LOST EVENTS

A complete record of discarded events would include races at what we would now regard as unusual lengths and various team races.

Baseball	1992–2008
Cricket	1900
Croquet	1900
Cross-country	1912, 1920–4
Discus (both hands)	1912
Discus (Greek-style)	1908
Golf	1900–1904
	(will be revived in 2016)
Ice Hockey	1920
Javelin (both hands)	1912
Jeu de paume (tennis without racquets)	
	1908
Lacrosse	1904–1908
Motor boating	1908
Pelota Basque	1900
Plunge for distance	1904
Polo	1900, 1908, 1920–1924, 1936
Rackets	1908
Roque (variation of croquet)	1904
Rugby Union	1900, 1908, 1920–1924
	(Rugby Sevens will be introduced in 2016)
Shot put (both hands)	1912
Softball	1996–2008
Standing high jump	1900–1912
Standing long jump	1900–1912
Standing triple jump	1900–1904
Steeplechase	1900
Stone throw	1906
Swimming obstacle race	1900
Tug of War	1900–1920
Walking	1906–1924, 1948–1952

A long way down

Another strange and short-lived water event was introduced at the 1904 Games – the plunge for distance. Competitors had to leap into the pool (yes, there was one in St Louis), sinking as deep as they could manage and then remaining motionless for 60 seconds or until their head broke the surface. (The American William Dickey won it, at 62 ft 6 in / 19.05 m.)

Look, no hands!

In those far-off days there was a much greater deference to those in authority. The American athlete Thomas P. Curtis later recalled a surprising experience while lining up for the 100-metre dash in 1896.

'Entered in the heat with me were a German, a Frenchman, an Englishman and two Greeks. As we stood on our marks, I was next to the Frenchman, a short, stocky man. He, at that moment, was busily engaged in pulling on a pair of white kid gloves, and having some difficulty in doing so before the starting pistol. Excited as I was, I had to ask him why he wanted the gloves. "Ah-ha!" he answered, "zat is because I run before ze Keeng!"'

Look, one leg!

The 33-year-old gymnast George Eyser entered the 1904 Olympics in St Louis at something of a disadvantage: as a young man he'd lost his left leg after being run over by a railway train.

His wooden leg proved not to be as much of a handicap as you'd have imagined, though. These were the first Games in which gold, silver and bronze medals were awarded, and Eyser picked up no fewer than three golds, two silvers and a bronze in a single day. One of his golds was for the vault, which involved jumping over a long horse without the aid of a springboard.

A very long haul

Apart from a break in 1900, wrestling has always been on the Olympic menu, but at Stockholm in 1912 it was the Greco-Roman version rather than freestyle which held sway. In this discipline (all the rage in Scandinavia just then) a wrestler wasn't allowed to use his legs to bring his opponent down, and no holds were allowed below the waist. That led to some seriously yawn-inducing bouts.

The light-heavyweight final between a Finn and a Swede lasted a full nine hours in sweltering heat before it was clear that neither athlete could muster the strength to win it. (Presumably whatever crowds there'd been at the beginning of the contest had now found more interesting things to do.) The judges declared the bout a draw, and both men were awarded silver medals.

But that was a brisk encounter compared with the middleweight semi-final between Russia's Martin Klein and Alfred 'Alpo' Asikainen of Finland. This lasted for eleven hours and forty minutes, with the wrestlers stopping for drinks every half-hour. This one did have a result, with Klein at last pinning his opponent – but he'd exhausted himself so much that he couldn't haul his weary frame to the final. (The gold went to Claes Johanson of Sweden by default.)

The oldest ever . . .
Oscar Swahn's record as the oldest medal winner in Olympic history is never likely to be be beaten. A marksman from Sweden, he took part in three consecutive Games.

• 1908: A mere 60-year-old, he wins two golds and a bronze in the running deer shooting events.

• 1912: At 64 years, 258 days he becomes the oldest gold medallist ever, as a member of the single shot running deer team. (He won a bronze, too.)

• 1920: Now 72, he's the oldest competitor of all time and, thanks to a silver in the double shot running deer contest, also the oldest medallist of all time. Beat that!

. . . and the youngest

If you go by the official records, then the youngest ever winner in the modern Olympics was the Greek gymnast Dimitris Loundras, who was part of the Greek team which came third in the team parallel bars event in 1896. Dimitris was just 10 years 218 days old – and it's a crying shame to spoil the story by pointing out that third place also happened to be *last* place that year.

Unofficially a much younger lad has that claim to fame, although sadly we don't know his name. During the delightfully named 'pair-oared shell with coxswain' competition in

1900 the Dutch rowers Antoine Brandt and Roelof Klein finished some way behind their French opponents in their qualifying heat, despite being hot favourites.

Why? Because they'd had an adult cox on board, whereas the French (quite legally) had used a young boy. For the final, the Dutch themselves found a local waif so light that they had to attach a lead weight to their rudder in order to force it under the water. *Touché!* They won the race by 0.2 seconds.

The young hero of the hour, who looked about seven years old, posed for a photograph with the triumphant pair – and then disappeared from Olympic glory for ever.

A meal too far
If wearing white gloves to run before a king was a tad obsequious, changing the time of an event to suit his social arrangements was simply outrageous. That's what happened at Antwerp in 1920. The final of the 10,000 metres was brought forward from 5.30pm to 2.15pm so that the King of Belgium could visit an art exhibition after handing out the medals.

This was particularly difficult for the French runner Joseph Guillemot, because nobody told him about the change until he'd finished tucking into a healthy lunch. A few days earlier Guillemot had beaten the great Finnish athlete Paavo Nurmi in the 5,000 metres – now he had to attempt a repeat performance over the longer distance weighed down by all that grub.

There was a terrific climax to the race, with Nurmi surging past the Frenchman on the final bend for a narrow win – whereupon Guillemot, going across to congratulate him, was sick all over the Finn's running shoes.

A MAN'S WORLD

You may have noticed that so far there's been no mention of a woman athlete in this sprint through the early modern Olympics. Pierre de Coubertin was an intelligent and thoughtful character, but his views about women in sport wouldn't have caused surprise in ancient Greece. They had grace and beauty, he thought, but they lacked both strength and the competitive spirit.

THE REMARKABLE BABE

This is the place to celebrate the achievements of the American athlete Mildred 'Babe' Didrikson (1913–56), an astonishing all-rounder who excelled at basketball, baseball, billiards, tennis, swimming and golf as well as the full range of track and field events.

Having qualified for all five individual women's events in the 1932 Olympics, she was allowed to compete in only three of them. She won the hurdles and the javelin and set a world record in the high jump – being denied victory because the judges didn't approve of her 'western roll' style (which was declared legal soon afterwards).

After that she devoted herself to golf, becoming the first American woman to win the British amateur title and, after turning professional, winning 33 tournaments, including the U.S. Open three times. She also found time to write the book *Championship Golf* in 1948.

Widely considered to be the greatest woman athlete of modern times, she was once asked if there were any games she didn't play.

'Yeah,' she replied in her lazy Texan drawl. 'Dolls.'

There were no women competitors at all in the 1896 Games, after which they began to make an appearance in events such as croquet, tennis, archery, swimming and diving.

The breakthrough came after Coubertin stepped down as IOC president in 1925. At the next Olympics (Amsterdam, 1928) women were at last allowed to compete in gymnastics and track and field competitions.

The end of the story? By no means! Coubertin, after all, wasn't the only diehard in the world of athletics. When several finalists in the 800 metres collapsed with exhaustion after their race, the new IOC president, the Belgian aristocrat Henri de Baillet-Latour, called for all women's events to be eliminated from the Olympic programme. Athletic competition, he pronounced, produced unfeminine women.

The IOC now obediently introduced a wholesale ban on women taking part in field and track events, only to back down when the United States threatened to boycott the 1932 Games – on its home soil.
Even some supporters of the women's cause

took a patronising attitude towards them. The Olympic sprint champion Harold Abrahams, who thought they should be allowed to take part, attributed their breakdowns in races to psychological rather than physical frailty: 'For reasons not instantly clear to the masculine understanding,' he wrote, 'they will cry when they win, and they will cry when they are beaten.'

OLGA HAD ALWAYS SAID, "IF I EVER SEE A MAN WITH A PISTOL, I'LL RUN A MILE."

Baillet-Latour's views were commonplace. The London *Daily Mail* said that women who took part in such 'feats of endurance' as 800 metres were in danger of becoming 'too old too soon', while a *Daily Telegraph* commentator thought that 'to run roughly half a mile at breakneck speed is surely too much for any girl.'

These critics got their way – the international athletics organisation, the IAAF, responded by banning races beyond 200 metres, and no women's Olympics event longer than that would be staged again until the Games in Rome 32 years later.

FOR LOVE, NOT MONEY

Amateurism was Coubertin's overriding ideal, and the IOC defended it fiercely – before, at last, it was seen to be a nonsense.

Pity the Italian Carlo Airoldi, who set off from Milan at the end of February 1896 to take part in the inaugural marathon, which he had a good chance of winning. He first *walked* some 700 miles to Ragusa in Yugoslavia at an average speed of 70 km (43 miles) a day, before taking a boat via Corfu to Patrasso and then walking a further 136 miles to Athens – along railway lines, as there were no roads. This slog had taken him more than a month, and yet when he handed in his entry form at the royal palace he was turned away on the grounds that he was a professional. *Have a nice walk home, Carlo!*

The problem, it seems, wasn't the fact that *La Bicicletta* magazine was paying his travelling costs in return for news of his exploits, but that the previous year he'd won the arduous Milano–Barcellona race (1050 km / 652 miles over 12 legs) and had taken home a cash prize.

Pity, too, the American Jim Thorpe, described by King Gustav V of Sweden as 'the greatest athlete in the world' after he won both the pentathlon and the decathlon at the Stockholm Games in 1912.

He returned home to the proverbial hero's welcome, leading a ticker-tape parade in New York, and said afterwards, 'I couldn't realise how one fellow could have so many friends.'

THAT OLYMPIC SPIRIT

Winning wasn't the most important thing, Coubertin said – and here are a few examples of athletes who shared that philosophy:

- When the Greek cyclist Georgios Kolettis had to stop to make repairs to his bike during the 100km track race in 1896, his sole opponent, the Frenchman Léon Flameng, immediately dismounted to wait for him. Virtue was rewarded, as Flameng went on to win the 300-lap race by a full eleven laps.

- The Australian oarsman Henry Pearce was flat out in the quarter-finals of the single sculls in 1928 when he realised that he was on collision course in the water with a mother duck and her ducklings. Pearce kindly stopped rowing to give them safe passage. Fortunately he still got through to the semi-finals, and eventually won the gold.

- The American discus thrower Al Oerter survived a terrible car crash to appear in the 1960 Olympics. Had that affected his stance? With only one round of throws left he trailed his great rival and fellow American 'Rink' Babka, whereupon Babka generously told him that he'd noticed his left arm was in the wrong position when he threw. Oerter gratefully accepted this advice – instantly breaking the Olympic record and claiming the gold medal.

You can imagine the shock a few months later when he was stripped of his titles because it was discovered that he had earned 25 dollars a week in 1909 and 1910 for playing minor league baseball in North Carolina. That made him a professional.

Thorpe wrote a desperate letter to the authorities, saying that he had been offered thousands of dollars since his Olympic triumphs, 'but I have turned them all down because I did not care to make money from my athletic skill'. It did him no good, because the American Olympic Committee demanded that he be punished, and the IOC ordered the return of his medals and trophies.

This story has a happy ending, although he didn't live to hear it. In 1982 the IOC decided that its treatment of Thorpe had been unfair. His name was returned to the record books, and his gold medals were presented to his children.

LOST AND FOUND

The Olympic flag, displaying the famous interlocking rings, was first flown at the Antwerp Games in 1920. There was a minor panic before the next Olympics, in Paris, when it was discovered to have flown in the other sense of the word – it was nowhere to be found and a new one had to be stitched in a hurry.

The mystery of the missing flag was at last solved more than 70 years later at an Olympic banquet. A reporter happened to mention its unaccountable disappearance to the American Haig 'Harry' Prieste, who'd won the bronze medal for platform diving at Antwerp.

'I can help you with that,' he said quietly. Prieste admitted that he'd climbed the flagpole at the end of the Games and taken the trophy home in his suitcase – and that's where it still lay all those years later.

Not only was Prieste forgiven for his escapade, but he became a minor celebrity. At the age of 103 he returned the flag at a special ceremony during the 2000 Sydney Games. The IOC president, Juan Antonio Samaranch, in turn presented him with a commemorative Olympic medal.

You can see the lost-and-found flag today in the Olympic Museum at Lausanne.

Perhaps the most farcical spat over supposed professionalism occurred at the Barcelona Olympics in 1992. The British 400 metres runner Phylis Smith had a good relationship with one of her local tradesmen in Wolverhampton, Arthur Cackett of Cackett's the Butchers ('established 1904').

He'd helped build up her strength by giving her some meat ('a nice bit of sirloin and a couple of turkey drumsticks,' is how he remembered it afterwards), and Smith was so grateful that she not only mentioned his name in an interview but scribbled the words 'Arthur Cackett hello' on her running bib before taking part in the semi-finals.

Her team manager was not amused, warning her of big trouble if she repeated the offence, while an IOC official promised to give her a ticking off about 'defacing her uniform'. She came last in the final.

But amateurism has many shades of grey. Even in ancient Greece the winning athletes were well rewarded, if not in prize money, and as the Games developed it was impossible for people without private means to devote time to serious training or afford the cost of travelling long distances to take part.

That's how it was in the modern Games, too. Strangely, Coubertin realised this unfairness himself, encouraging wealthy patrons to come foward to support working-class athletes – so what exactly were Arthur Cackett and Phylis Smith doing wrong?

Once national governments began to invest heavily in producing champion athletes it was a farce to pretend that all those extensively coached runners, jumpers and throwers were genuinely amateur on the grounds that they didn't actually receive a wage packet. And what about all those university scholarships awarded to supremely fit young men and women who didn't even pretend to shine academically?

THE OLYMPIC MUSEUM

Pierre de Coubertin fell in love with Lausanne, on the edge of Lake Geneva. He made it the headquarters of the IOC in 1915, lived there for long periods and founded the impressive Olympic Museum which today sits in attractive terraced grounds by the lake. He even encouraged the city to bid for the Olympics (unsuccessfully as it happened) five times between 1928 and 1960.

When he died in 1937 his body was buried in the city's Bois de Vaux cemetery, a mile or so from the museum, but his heart was taken away to be buried somewhere even more appropriate – at the site of the ancient Games in Olympia.

No, it couldn't go on – and after the 1988 Games the IOC voted to make all professionals eligible for the Olympics as long as the international federations in charge of each sport were happy with the idea. Boxing decided to remain amateur, and football to allow only three professionals in each national squad, but otherwise the old amateur/professional divide became a dead issue.

Did Baron Pierre de Coubertin perhaps turn (athletically) in his Bois de Vaux grave?

The famous Olympic symbol of five interlocking rings (blue, yellow, black, green and red) was devised by Pierre de Coubertin in 1912.

He said the rings represented 'the five parts of the world which now are won over to Olympism and willing to accept healthy competition'.

THE WINTER OLYMPICS

'We should never have created the Winter Olympic Games,' the IOC president Avery Brundage wrote in 1957, 'but how can we stop them now?'

It's strange to think that this exciting offspring of the Olympic movement should have caused such a stir, but it's always been dogged by one controversy or another.

Although figure skating and ice hockey made appearances during the 1920 summer Olympics, the idea of creating a separate event was first opposed by the Scandinavian countries who feared that it would take the gloss off their own Nordic Games.

It entered stealthily via the back door. The French had been given permission to organise an 'international winter sports week' alongside the main Games in Paris in 1924, and this event at Chamonix was so successful that it was retrospectively declared the first official Winter olympics.

Until 1992 the winter event was held in the same year as the summer one, but it had become so big (and was, in any case, so different) that from 1994 it began its own four-year cycle, two years apart from the main Olympics.

What Brundage didn't like about the Winter Olympics was that they were, from the start, more open to commercial influences than the summer Games – although today's vast corporate sponsorship and the sale of television rights were yet to come.

Fortunately he didn't live long enough to witness a scandal which first came to light in 1998, when it was revealed many IOC members had been bribed to give the Winter Games to Salt Lake City in 2002. Four of them resigned and six were expelled.

The Winter Olympics have also had their fair share of the controversies experienced by the summer Games (doping, political influence and so on) and they still have one inexplicable women's rights item on their agenda.

In 1991 the IOC ruled that all new Olympic sports must be open to both men and women. Ski-jumping wasn't a new one, however – and for some unfathomable reason women still aren't allowed to take part. Expect the protests to continue until they are . . .

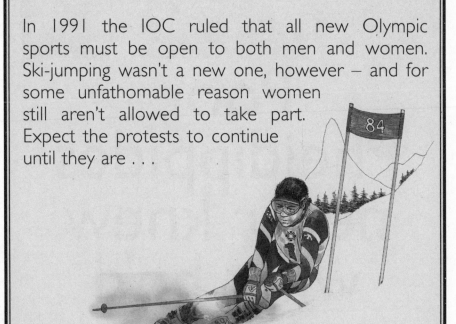

Poor Pheidippides never knew what he'd started.

THE MIGHTY MARATHON

In 490 BC, or so the story goes, the Greek soldier Pheidippides ran more than twenty miles non-stop along the mountain route from Marathon to Athens to report a miraculous victory over the Persians. He announced his stunning news to the gathered populace – and promptly dropped dead from exhaustion.

The ancient Greeks had no long-distance run in their Olympics, but a Robert Browning poem based on the legend ('Joy in his blood bursting his heart') inspired the founders of the modern Games to invent the messenger's gruelling 'tribute race', the marathon.

Many a long-distance runner must have pondered Pheidippides' fate when 'hitting the wall' a few miles from the finishing line. It's the unremitting slog of running for mile after mile in all conditions that makes the marathon such a special, dramatic event.

THE PRIDE OF GREECE

That first Olympic marathon from Marathon to Athens on 10 April 1896 caught the public's imagination to a startling degree – especially in Greece itself. One of Coubertin's friends, the French historian and linguist Michel Bréal, had a special cup made for the winner, and the wealthy local collector Ionnis Lambros more than matched that by putting up an antique vase depicting a runner in the ancient Games.

Other incentives included clothing, wine, a vast amount of chocolate (from the owner of a chocolate factory) and free haircuts for life at a local barber's. The Games' benefactor, Georgios Avroff, topped the lot by offering his daughter's hand in marriage plus a dowry of a million drachmas. Amateurism?!

Two trial marathons for Greek athletes were

held along the same course in the weeks before the Olympics. The first was won by Charilaos Vasilakos and the second (regarded as an official time trial) by Ioannis Laventis in 3hrs 11min 27sec. A humble water carrier named Spiridon Louis came fifth, exactly seven minutes behind, and he was swiftly recruited to the national team. The Greeks, having achieved little in the events prior to the marathon, were desperately pinning their hopes on one of their men coming home first.

Seventeen runners set off along the 40 km (25 mile) course – twelve from Greece, two from France, a Hungarian, an Australian and an American. Of the 'visitors' only Gyula Kellner of Hungary had run a comparable distance before, while three of the others had taken part in the 1500 metres on the previous day.

The Greek runners knew how to pace themselves, biding their time while the relative sprinters burned themselves out. One of these was the 1500 metres winner Edwin Flack, an Australian accountant, who led the race towards the end and was so confident of victory that he sent a cyclist ahead to let the

HOW THEY RAN THEN

A few incidents from the 1904 marathon in St Louis highlight the difference between the early 'come as you are' Olympics and today's intensely organised affair.

- Len Taunyane and Jan Mashiani were the first black Africans to take part in the Olympics, and they were joined by their white compatriot Bob Harris. They weren't, however, sent to America in order to compete in the Games. All three were part of a doubtful entertainment at the World's Fair, acting out two famous battles from the recent Boer War. As they were in St Louis, why not take part in the marathon?

- The race was badly organised, run on dusty roads and including no fewer than seven hills. Taunyane finished 9th and Mashiana 12th – but he would surely have done better if he hadn't been chased a mile off course by a wild dog.

- The Cuban postman Felix Carvajal lost all his money in a crap game in New Orleans while on the way to the Games. He hitch-hiked to St Louis and arrived at the starting line in his street clothes, beret and all. (Someone had cut off his trousers at the knee for him.) He was seized with stomach pains after stopping during the race to pick apples in an orchard – but still managed to come home in fourth place.

crowd in the stadium know he was on his way. Soon afterwards, however, he succumbed to exhaustion and became delirious. When a spectator came to his aid he thought he was being attacked – and punched him in the face. He promptly dropped out of the race and was given a drink of egg and brandy to bring him round.

Spiridon Louis, meanwhile, was equally optimistic, but with greater reason. While still lying sixth he paused for a glass of wine and told spectators 'Everything is going to plan'.

And so it was. One by one he passed his faltering opponents, coming into the stadium minutes ahead of Vasilakos in second place. 'It seemed that all of Greek antiquity entered with him,' Coubertin later wrote rather gushingly in his memoirs.

Louis, who became such a national hero that many stadiums are named after him today, now retired to a quiet life in his home village of Maroussi. He presented the antique vase to a museum and, already married, politely declined the offer of a new bride. When the king asked him to choose a reward befitting a national icon, Louis knew exactly what would be most useful to him – a donkey and cart to help him carry his water supplies from Maroussi to Athens.

TAKEN FOR A RIDE

Anyone who has tried to shorten the agony of a school cross-country run by finding a gap in the hedge will be tempted to sympathise with the Greek runner Spiridon Belokas, who came third in the inaugural marathon in 1896.

He seemed to have assured Greece a clean sweep of the podium positions, until Gyula Kellner, who had followed him into the stadium, revealed the uncomfortable truth – Belokas had travelled part of the way in a carriage. (He confessed and was disqualified.)

He wasn't, unfortunately, the last to try it on. Eight years later, in St Louis, Thomas Hicks, an English-born brass worker from Massachusetts, found himself in the lead with ten miles to go, but wilting in the heat of the afternoon. His back-up man gave him injections of strychnine and a disgusting cocktail of raw egg mixed with brandy, and Hicks was able to struggle on, though close to collapse.

Shortly before the end he was passed by the American Fred Lorz, who had a surprising spring in his step as he negotiated the final two hills of the course and eventually came home 15 minutes ahead of Hicks.

He had his photograph taken with President Roosevelt's daughter Alice, and was just about to receive the gold medal when the truth came out – he'd dropped out after nine miles, hitched a ride in a car and, when it broke down, decided to carry on running after all.

Lorz, who said it was 'a practical joke' which he would have later admitted, was banned for life by the Amateur Athletic Union. Quite right, too, you might say – but the ban was quickly lifted, and Lorz went on to win the Boston Marathon the following year.

A NEAR-DEATH EXPERIENCE

Sometimes greater glory attaches to a gallant loser than to a worthy winner, and so it was at the 1908 marathon in London. Dorando Pietri, a small, moustachioed pastry cook from Capri, was virtually unknown outside his own country, but his name was about to become recognised throughout the world.

Running with a knotted white handkerchief on his head against the heat, Pietri found himself some four minutes behind the South African Charles Hefferon at the 20-mile stage. He was steadily making up ground, however, and Hefferon soon made the mistake of taking a glass of champagne by way of refreshment. He felt dizzy and got the cramps, and Pietri passed him a mile from the finish.

HOW LONG IS A MARATHON?

The length of a marathon varied in the early days, but it eventually came to be fixed at the distance run in the 1908 London Olympics.

It was an arbitrary length, chosen in deference to Queen Alexandra, the wife of Edward VII. The organisers thought the grounds of Windsor Castle would make an ideal starting point. The finishing line would be inside the new White City stadium, and where else but directly opposite the royal box?

The organisers had originally planned a course of 25 miles, but they ended up with one of precisely 26 miles, 385 yards – or 42.195 km.

Victory now seemed his for the taking, but as he crossed Wormwood Scrubs and approached the White City stadium, the oppressive heat of a midsummer afternoon began to sap his strength. The crowd of 100,000 watched him falter as he descended the ramp to the cinder track – turning the wrong way, and having to be redirected by the officials. He scarcely knew where he was.

Anyone who has watched Pietro's distress on film can never forget it. He tottered on, collapsed to the ground and scrambled to his feet as doctors and officials ran to help him. Three more times he fell, each time forcing himself to stand once more. Fifty yards from the tape he attempted a last sprint, but he crumpled to the ground while still ten yards short of it.

The official report of the Games later claimed 'it was impossible to leave him there, for it looked as if he might die in the very presence of the Queen'. (Never mind anyone else!)

OLYMPIC BESTS *

MARATHON

Men:
Samuel Wanjiru (Kenya)
2:06:32   2008 Beijing

Women:
Tiki Gelana (Ethiopia)
2:23:07 2012 London

* All records in this book include the 2012 Games. They are not necessarily world records.

With this in mind, no doubt, the chief race organiser helped him to cross the line.

Stretchered away, and apparently close to death – 'My heart had moved half an inch out of place with the strain of the run,' he said afterwards. 'They brought me back to life by massaging my heart into place.' – Pietri had the gold medal snatched away after the Americans protested (correctly) that being helped should disqualify him.

Never mind, Queen Alexandra was so impressed by his bravery that she presented him with a special gold cup inscribed 'In remembrance of the Marathon Race from Windsor to London'.

PICNIC TIME

Another marathon non-winner who won himself a later fame of sorts was the Japanese runner Shizo Kanakuri.

The 1912 event at Stockholm was yet again held in stifling heat (34 runners failed to finish), and Kanakuri had trouble coping with it. With his legs almost gone, he veered off the road and into the garden of a family who were enjoying a summer picnic. With typical Swedish hospitality, they invited him to join them. After sinking copious glasses of raspberry juice he lay down for a nap – and woke too late to continue in the race.

Humiliated, Kanakuri took a train to Stockholm and caught a boat back to Japan. The trouble was that he didn't tell anyone he was going. When the organisers did their post-race tally of all the runners they felt obliged to call in the police to trace him, and he was officially listed as a 'missing person'.

The end of the affair? By no means! Unknown to Kanakuri himself, he had become a cult

Shizo thought the marathon was a piece of cake.

figure in Sweden, with many unlikely reported sightings of him and suggestions that he was still pounding the streets in search of the stadium. He became a figure of folklore. On the fiftieth anniversary of the race, the Swedish journalist Oscar Söderland was sent to Japan to track him down – apparently unaware that, far from being in hiding, Kanaguri had taken part in the next two Olympics after Stockholm and was regarded in Japan as 'the father of the marathon'.

DEATH IN THE AFTERNOON

Perhaps it was surprising that it hadn't happened before, but in the heat of Stockholm in 1912 the Portuguese record holder, 21-year-old Francisco Lázaro, keeled over and died after completing 18 miles (29 km) of the marathon.

Lázaro, who had claimed the course was much easier than the one he was used to running in his mountains at home, had covered his body in wax to prevent sunburn, and it's thought that this eventually led to severe dehydration.

A monument was placed at the marathon's turning point at Sollentuna, and a public collection raised a large sum for his widow.

In 1966 the good-natured runner, now in his seventies, agreed to return to the city to complete his run.

His time as he crossed the finishing line, to the delight of an adoring Swedish public, was 54 years, 8 months, 6 days, 8 hours, 32 minutes, 20.3 seconds.

A LITTLE OFF KEY

The first African winner of the Olympic marathon was the barefoot runner from Ethiopia, Abebe Bikila. A member of Emperor Haile Selassie's household guard, he had been inspired to take up running after watching his fellow countrymen appear in the 1956 Melbourne Games. Four years later, with only two (albeit fast) marathons under his belt, Bikila arrived in Rome as a complete unknown.

In what was the first ever night-time Olympic marathon, he kept pace with the front runners all the way, and by the closing stages was in a two-horse race with the Moroccan Rhadi ben

THE END OF CROSS-COUNTRY

Although the marathon survived calls for it to be abolished after Francisco Lázaro's death in Stockholm, its junior relative, the cross-country race, failed to survive the punishing conditions experienced by the 38 runners in Paris twelve years later.

They set off on one of the hottest days the capital had ever known, with temperatures reaching 45°C (113°F), and they found the course crucifyingly difficult. At one point they passed an energy plant pumping out poisonous fumes, and another stretch by the River Seine forced them to run through knee-high thistles.

Only fifteen of the athletes completed the course, and eight of those had to be carried away on stretchers. Out on the roads, vomiting athletes were collapsing with sunstroke, and it would take hours for the Red Cross and Olympic officials to account for them all. A Spaniard who fell and hit his head on a marker was taken to hospital, and two runners who collided near the finish found it impossible to pick themselves up and carry on.

The wonder among all this mayhem was that the great Paavo Nurmi, having won both the 1500 metres and 5000 metres two days before (with just an hour between them), cantered to the gold as if nothing untoward at all were happening behind him. Oh, and the next day, while the other cross-country runners licked their wounds, he won another gold in the 3000 metres team race.

Abdesellem. He had already decided where he would launch his sprint finish – by the ancient obelisk of Axum which the Italian army had looted from Ethiopia in 1937 during the fascist dictatorship of Benito Mussolini.

His plan worked like a dream, and Bikila came home a full eight minutes inside the Olympic record, setting a new world record into the bargain.

There was just one jarring note. Nobody had expected there to be a gold-medal winner from Ethiopia, which meant that the stadium band didn't have the music of its anthem. They played the Italian one instead.

BETTER LATE THAN NEVER

The Tanzanian Olympic Committee had struggled to finance sending three athletes to the 1968 Games in Mexico City, and one of them was the marathon runner John Akhwari.

With the Olympics held at an altitude of above 10,000 ft (3,000 metres), many of the athletes becan to feel dizziness and fatigue. Akhwari suffered severe cramp and spasms, and before the 20-mile mark he fell and gashed his right knee. His coach bandaged the wound, but when it was clear that his man could do little more than limp along he encouraged him to give up, telling him that he'd done enough and that everyone had already gone home.

Akhwari would have none of it. As he said afterwards, 'My country didn't send me 7,000 miles to start the race. They sent me 7,000 miles to finish it.'

And finish it he did – entering the stadium more than an hour behind the winner, breaking into a trot to cross the line and then collapsing in agony. He spent two weeks recuperating in a local clinic before going home amid huge media acclaim.

The film-maker Bud Greenspan, who trained his camera on Akhwari's defiant last steps to the finishing line, described this display of dogged courage as 'the greatest moment in Olympic history'.

NOT SO FAST!

A loser who certainly didn't win any acclaim was Apolinario 'Polin' Belisle Gómez. Born in Honduras, brought up in Belize and living in California, he was a would-be marathon star who lacked any natural aptitude but had a whole lot of (wayward) determination.

He did take part in a few marathons, but although he started and finished each one he never seemed to be picked up on the race videos throughout the miles in between. Somehow, though, he managed to be reported in a local newspaper as having posted a fast time in the Long Beach Marathon, and with this frail evidence in his hands he persuaded the Belizean Olympic committee to include him in their team for the 1988 Seoul Games.

This was a race Belisle did complete, although – without any excuse of illness or injury – he came an emphatic last in a time of 3:14:02, more than an hour behind the winner.

Was that the end of his Olympic career? He had other ideas! After Belize, not surprisingly, refused to give him another chance he got himself included in the Honduras Olympic squad at Barcelona four years later. Alas, someone recognised him, and the Hondurans promptly dropped him from the team.

Most of us would have slunk away in disgrace at this point, but Belisle was made of sterner stuff. The authorities had neglected to take away his identity card and race number, so Belisle turned up for the marathon and managed to infiltrate the first rank of runners.

Off they set, and for nearly a mile Belisle had his day, running shoulder to shoulder with the greatest long-distance runners in the world. Then, job done, and the pace no doubt telling, he slipped back into the following pack and quietly disappeared.

THE MUNICH JOKER

Polin Belisle wasn't the first Olympic marathon hoaxer, although Norbert Sudhaus's stunt at Munich in 1972 was a much briefer affair.

A 22-year-old German student, Sudhaus togged himself up in running gear (orange shorts and a blue vest with the number 72) and joined the route just ahead of the genuine runners half a mile from the finish. The cheering crowd in the stadium looked on amazed as officials grabbed the surprisingly fresh race leader along the back straight.

'These Games have been far too serious,' Sudhaus said afterwards. 'I thought they needed some cheering up.'

THAT OLYMPIC SPIRIT

We'll end the chapter with features of the 1996 Atlanta marathon which encapsulate the many sides of this incomparable event – the drama, the bravery, the occasional confusion and a strong dash of the Olympic spirit.

• Josia Thugwane was a poor, illiterate South African who, two weeks after qualifying for the Games, had been shot in the chin by men stealing his truck. The 25-year-old arrived in Atlanta quite unaware of the prestige of the Olympics. At 5 ft 2 in (1.58 m) and 7 stone (47 kg) he was the smallest of the 123 runners and was ranked 41st in the world by time – yet he took the marathon by storm, sprinting home a few seconds ahead of his nearest rival, having run the second half of the race faster than the first.

THE SCHEISS RULE

Women were at last given their own Olympic marathon at Los Angeles in 1984, and the race is best remembered for the agonising final lap of the stadium by the 39-year-old ski instructor Gaby Andersen–Scheiss, who was representing Switzerland. She staggered into view from the tunnel in obvious distress, but waved away all attempts to help her.

After a full 5 minutes and 44 seconds, sometimes blacking out on her feet, she fell across the finishing line in 37th place.

The drama led to the so-called 'Scheiss rule' which allows athletes to receive a medical examination without being disqualified.

Typically, he knew nothing about the award ceremony and had to be pointed to the stand to be given his medal – the first gold ever won by a black South African. He celebrated victory by buying himself a CD player and thirty CDs.

• Ethiopia's Turbo Tumo had no chance of winning, but as he entered the stadium in 60th place he was so befuddled by the intense heat (a familiar story), that he lost his bearings and wandered off the track without finishing.

• Islam Djugum of Bosnia-Herzogovina, who carried his national flag at the opening ceremony, was very lucky to be there. The sole member of the Bosnian team who had stayed in his country throughout the war with Yugoslavia, he had constantly changed the route of his training runs through the streets to avoid being the target of snipers. As it was, he had to stop more than once to help get the survivors of massacres to hospital.

• Abdul Baser Wasigi from Kabul in Afghanistan had missed the previous Olympics because of the chaos of war. This time he made it, but injured his hamstring shortly after arriving.

Wasigi's plucky run was reminiscent of John Akhwari's in 1968. Despite not being able to train he was determined to take part – and to finish. He had completed only 15 miles (25 km) when Thugwane breasted the tape, but on and on he limped, coming home in 4:24:17, the slowest time in Olympic history.

Failure? The closing ceremony was delayed to welcome him, hundreds lined the track to applaud him into the stadium, the band struck up a fanfare and a group of his new-found admirers wrote 'Atlanta 96' on white plastic tape and stretched it across the finishing line.

• And let's pay a final tribute to the good people of Hattiesburg, Mississippi, who took to their hearts the small contingent from Malawi – a country then so poor that it could afford to send no more than two athletes to the Games.

As soon as the runners John Mwathiwa and Henry Moyo arrived at their training base at the University of Southern Mississippi the locals realised that their running gear was threadbare and sparse. This state of affairs simply couldn't survive southern hospitality, and the community swiftly rallied round – buying them training shoes and gym bags, sewing them new uniforms, taking them on sight-seeing tours and inviting them to picnics and other events.

Local housewives thought the runners needed filling out and offered to fry up 'a mess of catfish', but the men plumped for the grits that were similar to their cornmeal diet at home.

When the men appeared in the stadium their tracksuits bore small labels which read 'Hattiesburg Convention and Visitors Bureau'.

John Mwathiwa duly took part in the marathon. It would be good to report that he finished in the medals, rather than in 65th place, but in this case the story itself is undoubtedly the happy ending.

THE PARALYMPIC GAMES

They began humbly enough in 1948 as a competition for war veterans in wheelchairs at the Stoke Mandeville rehabilitation hospital in Buckinghamshire, England. They evolved over time to become the second largest sporting event on earth – second, that is, only to the Olympic Games themselves.

The Paralympics (motto: 'Spirit in Motion') are held every two years in parallel with the summer and winter Olympics. Athletes compete in six broad categories – amputee, wheelchair, visually impaired, cerebral palsy, intellectual disability and Les Autres, which includes dwarfism, multiple sclerosis and congenital deformities.

THE BLADE RUNNER

South African Paralympic athlete Oscar Pistorius was known as 'the fastest man on no legs'.

Born without fibula bones, he had his legs amputated below the knee when just eleven months old, yet grew up insisting that he would be a sportsman. He played water polo, tennis and rugby – and then, in his teens, shattered his right knee in a rugby game.

An end to his dreams? Pistorius simply switched to track events and, after training for only two months, broke the world Paralympics 100 metres record. In 2007 he entered the South African national championships and won silver racing against able-bodied opponents.

A year later, running on his high-tech carbon-fibre 'blades', he became the first man to win gold in the 100, 200 and 400 metre Paralympic sprint events.

Those blades proved controversial, at one time being banned as giving him an unfair advantage. When the ban was lifted, Pistorius announced his ambition to take part in the main 2008 Olympics in Beijing. He entered the pre-Olympic trials in his home country, and only just missed out on a time fast enough to win him a place in the national team.

At the 2012 Summer Paralympics, Pistorius won gold medals in both the 400 metre and 4 x 100 metre relay races, and a silver medal in the 200 metre competition.

Pistorius subsequently received media notoriety when he was found guilty of culpable homicide after fatally shooting his girlfriend, Reeva Steenkamp. He is currently serving a five-year prison sentence.

Other international events for physically handicapped athletes include the World Wheelchair and Amputee Games and the Deaflympics, where thousands compete.

SOME OLYMPIC FIRSTS . . .

1896	First modern Olympic Games
1908	First national teams, with athletes marching behind their countries' flags
1912	Rudimentary photo-finish equipment
1920	First appearance of Olympic flag and oath
1924	First appearance of Olympic flame
1928	First photography rights sold to a commercial firm
1932	First winners' national anthems played; flags raised; Olympic village (men only); three-tiered victory stand
1936	First torch relay
1956	First political boycotts
1960	First world-wide TV transmission
1968	First gender testing
1972	First full-scale drug testing
1976	First anabolic steroid testing
1984	First 'private enterprise games' in Los Angeles, with vast corporate sponsorship
1988	First professionals admitted
1996	First Games (Atlanta) run without government support

RUNNING INTO TROUBLE

The ancient Greeks would have smiled at Coubertin's notion that taking part in the Games was more important than winning. So, too, would thousands of modern athletes for whom years of physical exertion can only be properly rewarded by taking home a medal.

The founder's beloved 'fair play' Olympics have grown into a monster of professionalism and commercialism. What would he make of athletes pumped up with drugs, IOC officials taking back-handers and governments and activists putting propaganda before sport?

HITLER'S GAMES

The most notorious use of the Olympics to suit a national agenda was the Hitler regime's staging of the 1936 Games in Berlin. The city had been chosen before the Nazis took over the country, but Coubertin's ideals of democracy and equality were blatantly at odds with the odious race prejudice which saw Jews banned from competing in the German team and 800 local Gypsies rounded up by the police and incarcerated in a special camp for the duration of the event.

OLYMPIA – THE FILM

Hitler's favourite film maker, Leni Riefenstahl, captured the 1936 Games on celluloid. Her two-part documentary *Olympia* was the first ever made about the Olympics, and because of its innovative techniques (including unusual angles, extreme close-ups and the use of cameras on rails to track the athletes) it's now regarded as a classic.

Some critics have condemned the film as propaganda, if only because it glorifies what was an obvious showcase for the Nazis, but Riefenstahl allowed no racial bias in reporting what her cameras saw.

Should the Games have been held somewhere else? Many thought so, but many more were persuaded that the hosts had listened to criticism and – in public at least – had toned down the worst of their rhetoric. Well, they even took down signs around the city which said things like 'Jews Not Wanted'.

In America – which itself had a shameful record on black rights – there was a fierce debate about whether sending a team to Berlin would be seen as encouraging the Hitler government. Avery Brundage (a member of the US Olympic Committee, who would later become the IOC president) managed to persuade the Amateur Athletic Union to vote, albeit narrowly, in favour of going.

Once teams arrived in Berlin they had to decide whether to give Hitler the Nazi salute inside the stadium. There was some confusion over which athletes had complied, because the Olympic salute (the right arm held out to the right sideways from the shoulder) wasn't unlike the German one. The Americans gave a 'hat over heart' gesture, while the British offered a simple eyes-right salute, neither of which went down very well with the crowd.

The black American Jesse Owens famously won four gold medals, to the great displeasure of the führer, who believed that 'negroes' were an inferior race. One heartening episode in these bad-taste-in-the-mouth Games came during the long jump, when Owens was publicly befriended by his close rival, the stereotypical tall, blonde, blue-eyed German, Luz Long.

Long openly offered his congratulations after being beaten into second place, and then walked arm-in-arm with him to the dressing room. 'You can melt down all the medals and cups I have,' Owens later wrote, 'and they wouldn't be a plating on the 24-carat friendship I felt for Luz Long at that moment.'

A less comfortable episode was the dropping of the Jewish sprinters Sam Stoller and Marty Glickman from the US 4x100 metre relay team on the very day of the competition. Glickman was convinced that Brundage and his colleagues had withdrawn the runners to

'THE SPORTIVE, KNIGHTLY BATTLE AWAKENS THE BEST HUMAN CHARACTERISTICS. IT DOESN'T SEPARATE, BUT UNITES THE COMBATANTS IN UNDERSTANDING AND RESPECT. IT ALSO HELPS TO CONNECT THE COUNTRIES IN THE SPIRIT OF PEACE. THAT'S WHY THE OLYMPIC FLAME SHOULD NEVER DIE.'

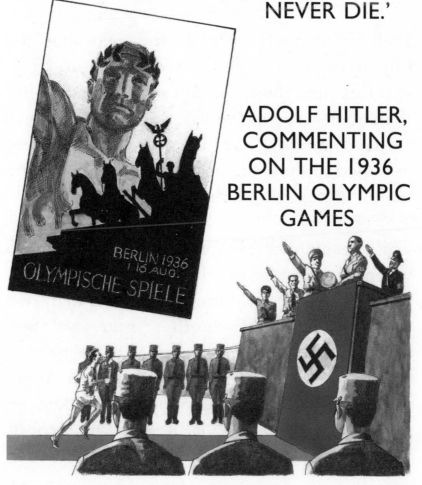

ADOLF HITLER, COMMENTING ON THE 1936 BERLIN OLYMPIC GAMES

appease Hitler's anti-semitism, and Stoller was so devastated that his immediate reaction was to retire from athletics. (He was later persuaded to change his mind.) The official line was that they were replaced because two of the black American runners, including Jesse Owens, were faster.

MURDER IN MUNICH

Politics intruded violently the next time the Olympics were held in Germany, in 1972, and this time the trouble was imported rather than home-grown. Indeed, the Munich Games (official motto, The Happy Games) were intended to show the best of a new, democratic nation at peace with itself.

This peace was shattered on September 5 when a group of Palestinian terrorists broke into the Olympic village, killed two Israelis and held another nine hostage. They demanded the release of prisoners by the Israeli government, and after tense negotiations they were offered safe passage out of the country via a military airport. The German authorities planned to ambush

THE TORCH RELAY

There was almost certainly a sacred flame at Olympia in ancient times, but the Olympic torch is a modern invention, first appearing at Amsterdam in 1928.

The torch relay from Greece to the Olympic stadium is more recent still – the Germans dreamed it up for the Berlin Games in 1936, and the theatrical impact of the flame being passed from runner to runner over thousands of miles made it a fixture. (You can see all the torches in the Olympic Museum in Lausanne.)

The honour of carrying the torch into the stadium to  light the Olympic Flame is usually awarded to a sports celebrity of the host country, but the choice sometimes has a deeper significance. At the 1964 Games in Tokyo, for example, the Flame was lit by the runner Yoshinori Sakai, who was born in Hiroshima on August 6 1945 – the day the atomic bomb Little Boy devastated the city – so symbolising Japan's post-war rebirth. And at Montreal in 1976 the unity of Canada was embodied in two teenagers, one from the English-speaking part of the country and the other from the French.

the terrorists, but the attempt was botched, and in the ensuing firefight 15 people were killed, including all nine Israeli athletes and five of the terrorists. The end of the Munich Olympics? Some thought their abandonment would be a fitting token of respect to those who had died, but Avery Brundage was among those who successfully argued that 'the Games must go on'. Depending on your point of view, this was either bravely defiant or basely cynical.

TARNISHED GOLD

James H. Snook, one of the 5-man US pistol team which won gold at the 1920 Olympics, later became head of the department of veterinary medicine at Ohio State University. His invention for spaying animals, the Snook Hook, is still used today.

Outside the animal world, however, Professor Snook is remembered for something much more sombre. In June 1929 he brutally murdered one of his students, Theora Hix – using not a Snook Hook but a hammer and a knife.

He became the only Olympic gold medallist to be executed in the electric chair.

STAYING AT HOME

The fact is that an event as vast as the Games is irresistible to protesters of all kinds – and boycotting them has long proved a handy way for governments to make political points.

Here's a selection of stay-aways and the grounds for their absence:

- 1956, Melbourne
    Netherlands, Spain, Switzerland: the Soviet repression of the Hungarian uprising
    Cambodia, Egypt, Iraq, Lebanon: the Suez Crisis
    China: Taiwan being allowed to compete

- **1976, Montreal**
    20 African countries, Guyana, Iraq: A New Zealand rugby team had toured South Africa
    Taiwan: Not being allowed to compete as The Republic of China

- **1980, Moscow**
  66 nations, led by the USA: The
  Soviet invasion of Afghanistan

- **1984, Los Angeles**
  Soviet Union and 14 Eastern Bloc
  countries: Unable to guarantee the
  safety of their athletes in America

BLACK POWER

The 1968 Mexico City Games looked set to be boycotted by a large number of black athletes, until the IOC agreed to ban South Africa and Rhodesia because of their apartheid policies.

An American organisation called the Olympic Project for Human Rights (OPHR) had condemned the treatment of black people in the United States (where the civil rights leader Dr Martin Luther King had recently been assassinated), asking 'Why should we run in Mexico, only to crawl home?'

The OPHR demanded the removal of Avery Brundage as head of the US Olympic

Committee for having supported South Africa's entry to the Olympic movement in the first place, and also called for the restoration of Muhammad Ali's world boxing title, which had been stripped from him after he refused to fight in the Vietnam war.

Although the South Africa ban defused the boycott, several black American athletes were determined to make a protest in Mexico. Brundage warned that any of them who demonstrated would be sent home – to which a group of them replied that they didn't want Brundage presenting them with medals as IOC president.

Their moment came at the medals ceremony for the 200 metres (with Lord Exeter presenting them rather than the unwelcome Brundage). Tommie Smith, who had won gold in a world record time, and John Carlos, who had taken the bronze, bowed their heads while The Star-Spangled Banner anthem was played, and then each raised a black-gloved hand in the Black Power salute.
Both men wore black socks with no running shoes (as a reminder of black poverty in the

United States, they later explained), while Smith wore a black scarf (black pride) and Carlos a string of beads (in honour of black Americans who had been lynched). Both men wore OPHR badges, as also did the Australian Peter Norman, who had won the silver medal: he said he opposed the whites-only immigration policy in his own country.

THE BLACK POWER SALUTE

The IOC response to this dramatic, but harmless, protest was inevitable. It said that unless the US Olympic Committee agreed to ban Smith and Carlos, the entire US track and field team would be sent home too. (They caved in.)

Although their fellow American Olympic athletes, white as well as black, came out in their support, the two men found their lives ruined when they arrived back in the United States. The media were overwhelmingly against them, their familes received death threats and they found it hard to get decent jobs as athletics coaches.

Carlos afterwards took issue with the idea that his protest had tainted the Games with politics. They were already deeply political, he said: 'Why do you have to wear the uniform of your country? Why do they play national anthems? Why do we have to beat the Russians? What happened to the Olympic ideal of man against man?'

And how, we might ask, would Pierre de Coubertin have answered those questions?

THE FAKE TORCH

What the lord mayor of Sydney, Pat Hills, didn't realise as he graciously received the Olympic torch during its long journey to Melbourne was that what he held in his hands was a sawn-off broom handle and an old jam tin stuffed with a pair of underpants.

A group of Australian university students, deciding that the nation's 1956 Olympic fervour was ridiculously over-the-top, had painted their device silver, soaked the underwear with kerosene and applied a match. Twenty-year-old Barry Larkin then set off some way ahead of the genuine torch, and found himself jogging along the road flanked by an escort of police motorcycles while a cheering crowd urged him on.

Never expecting to have got so far, Larkin now found himself at the foot of the town hall steps, thinking (as he said later) 'What am I going to do now?'

What he did was present the flaming jam tin to the mayor, walk back down the steps and jump on a tram. The mayor gave his speech, the crowd dispersed — and then (oh, dear!) the real torch arrived . . .

LOOK AT ME!

Individual attention-grabbing stunts at the Olympics haven't always had the seriousness or resonance of the Black Power protest.

• During the men's synchronised diving at Athens in 2004 spectators were astounded to see a man dressed in a blue tutu and white tights with polka dots step onto the three-metre board and leap into the water with a cry of 'I love you!'

It appeared that the 31-year-old Canadian Ron Bensimhon wasn't deranged, but was advertising an on-line gaming site. (He was given a five-month jail sentence.) Meanwhile the Chinese athletes who were in the lead when Bensimhon gate-crashed the event were so distracted that they produced a no-dive and fell to last place.

• Security clearly wasn't tight in Athens, because the marathon was interrupted by a man in a red kilt and green beret who carried a white placard reading, 'The Grand Prix Priest – the Second Coming is Near'.

This was the defrocked Irish priest Cornelius Horan, who burst onto the course some four miles from the finish and hustled the race leader, the Brazilian Vanderleide Lima, off the road. Lima was overtaken a couple of miles later, eventually coming home in third place, and he blamed the assault for ruining his rhythm and concentration.

Horan, regarded as mentally unstable (he'd run across the Grand Prix track at Silverstone the previous year), was later fined and given a suspended sentence. Lima, having been denied the gold, was awarded the Pierre de Coubertin Medal for an 'exceptional demonstration of fair play and Olympic values during this evening's marathon' – a small consolation, no doubt.

BAD BLOOD

Unfortunately we can't blame all Olympic unpleasantness on politicians or individual interlopers. Most athletes accept defeat with good grace, but the history of the Games is littered with ill-mannered spats between the competitors themselves.

• In 1900 the two American long jumpers Alvin Kraenzlein and Myer Prinstein came to blows after a final in which Prinstein (who had recently taken the world record from his opponent) didn't compete. That was because it was held on a Sunday: Syracuse University, which had sent him to Paris, didn't allow its athletes to take part on the Lord's Day.

Prinstein went along with this despite being Jewish, and he assumed that Kraenzlein, a Christian, would do the same. You can imagine his fury when Kraenzlein turned up for the final and won it. The two men remained sworn enemies for life.

• The 400 metres in London in 1908 wasn't run in lanes, and the British finalist Wyndham Halswelle knew he had to watch out for his three American opponents – John Carpenter, John Taylor and William Robbins – because they were used to a more rough-house kind of event in their own country.

He was right to be worried, because as he powered down the home straight towards the finishing line Carpenter cut right across him at a sharp angle, using his elbows and all but forcing him off the track. The judges quickly broke the tape to abandon the race and the furious Taylor had to be dragged away by officials as the British and Americans traded choice insults for a full half-hour.

When it was decided to re-stage the race two days later without Carpenter, the other Americans refused to take part, and Halswelle had to be persuaded to run on his own for an unopposed gold.

The *New York Press* accused the British of being bad losers, claiming that 'our uncousinly competitors have to learn how to win from American athletes, and they still more need to learn how to lose'.

What the IOC learned from this debacle was that judges should be selected from an international pool rather than solely from the host nation in order to prevent charges of favouritism. Meanwhile the International Amateur Athletics Assocation was set up in 1912 to standardise the rules – and American-style interference on the track was banned.

SABRES AT DAWN

There was such ill-feeling between the Italians and Hungarians during the 1924 fencing tournament that two real duels were fought once the Games were over.

One was between the Hungarian referee Gyorgy Kovacs and the Italian fencer Oreste Puliti, who was disqualified from the sabre event after threatening to cane Kovacs for remarks he had made. Their duel is said to have lasted for an hour, with some blood shed on both sides before hands were shaken and honour was satisfied.

The other featured two Italians. Italo Santelli was the Hungarian fencing coach, and he fell out with the Italian captain, Adolfo Contronei. Since Santelli was too old for a fair fight, his son Giorgio stood in for him.

Many years later Giorgio's memory of the duel was that they fenced for about three minutes, until he struck Contronei on the side of the head: 'He was temporarily blinded, and so the duel was stopped. He required 12 stitches.'

The two men met again at the 1932 Olympics – and had dinner together.

• When the Czech team reached the football final against the home nation, Belgium, in 1920 they weren't best pleased to discover that the referee would be the Englishman John Lewis who had been physically assaulted by disgruntled Czech fans only a few months earlier.

They were even less pleased when he awarded a penalty against them after only ten minutes and then sent one of their players off – quite reasonably, as he'd just kicked a Belgian in the chest. The incensed Czech players now

A RACE WITH DEATH

Dieudonné Lamothe was well out of the running in the Los Angeles marathon in 1984 – so far behind the rest of the pack that you might have expected him to make a tactful withdrawal.

Still the Haitian kept going, though, finally crossing the line not only last of the 78 finishers but a full 43 minutes behind the winner.

What had kept him going? His explanation was readily understood. The brutal Haitian dictator Baby Doc Duvalier had assured him that if he failed to finish the race he would be killed – and Lamothe knew he was the kind of man who meant it.

walked off the pitch and refused to return, so handing the gold medal to their opponents.

After this unpleasantness there were calls for Britain to withdraw from future Games on the grounds that they were no longer conducted in a sporting manner. They hadn't seen anything yet!

• The Paris Olympics in 1924 had more than their fair share of unpleasant behaviour. For one thing the French crowds took to booing the national anthems of other countries, which hardly encouraged a spirit of goodwill.

Bad feeling seemed to spread like a miasma. When the defending middleweight boxing champion, London policeman Harry Mallin, was beaten on points in the quarter-finals by the local bruiser Roger Brousse, he not only contested the result (most observers thought he had won easily) but pointed out bite marks on his body.

The London *Daily Sketch* fulminated, 'It was found necessary to substitute for a mere boxer a man-eating expert named Brousse, whose passion for raw meat led him to attempt to bite off portions of his opponents' anatomies.'

The Olympic appeal jury disqualified Brousse, despite deciding that the biting hadn't been deliberate, and Mallin went on to take gold again in front of a hostile French crowd.

The English referee T.H. Walker, meanwhile, found himself pelted with coins, sticks and walking stick knobs after disqualifying an Italian boxer, and he was trapped in the arena for about an hour before making his escape.

Events turned even more ugly on the rugby pitch. The visiting American team wasn't expected to win, but its players were big and tough, and when they were held up at immigration in Boulogne they brushed the authorities aside and forced their way ashore.

Their reputation as uncivilised thugs was cemented when – given only a patch of scrubland to exercise on – they similarly forced their way into the near-sacred Stade Colombes and did their training there. By now they were hate figures, spat upon whenever they appeared in public.

The match itself was a bone-jarring affair, and the strength of the Americans soon began to prove decisive. This was too much for the raucous French crowd, which began to beat up any American supporters it could find, their unconscious bodies being lowered through the stands to the side of the pitch.

'I thought they were dead,' the American player Norman Cleaveland said afterwards. 'They were throwing bottles and rocks, and clawing at us through the fence. We were sure it was only a matter of time before they got their hands on us.'

The Times newspaper called for 'No More Olympic Games', saying that 'the peace of the world is too precious to justify any risk, however wild the idea may seem, of its being sacrificed on the altar of international sport'.

• December 1956 wasn't a good time for a sporting fixture between teams from Hungary and the Soviet Union, because only weeks previously Russian tanks had swept into Hungary to crush its revolution against Communist rule.

All the animosity between the two countries seemed to be concentrated in a violent, no-holds-barred skirmish in the water polo pool. The first punch was apparently thrown by a Hungarian while scoring the first of their four goals, but after that it was a water-churning melee of kicks, scratches and punches until the referee – who had already sent off three Russians and a Hungarian – decided to end the match early.

Hungary's Ervin Zador, taken to hospital with blood pouring from around his right eye, announced the verdict: 'It wasn't water polo. It was a boxing match underwater.'

The aquarium's latest exhibit was a smash hit.

ILLEGAL SUBSTANCES

Cheating comes in many guises, but the use of performance-enhancing drugs is the most common form of it – and the one which the IOC spends most time and money trying to eradicate. It's engaged in an unending battle of wits with unscrupulous athletes, coaches and doctors who use every trick in the book – including masking agents – to avoid the detection of stimulants, sedatives, steroids, hormones and even genetic modification

VICIOUS CYCLE

The danger of taking drugs was highlighted on a steamingly hot Rome day in August 1960 when the 23-year-old Danish cyclist Knut Jensen crashed and died during the gruelling 62-mile team race at the Cristoforo Colombo circuit – the first Olympics death since the 1912 marathon.

Jensen, who was the Scandinavian road racing champion, came off his bike 13 miles from the finish, fracturing his skull. The heat had undoubtedly taken its toll, but tests revealed that he had taken the banned blood circulation stimulant Ronicol before the race, and that this had contributed to his collapse.

through the use of increasingly sophisticated scientific laboratory techniques.

The most horrific wholesale administration of drugs to athletes occured in the former East Germany during the 1970s – horrific because many of the young female athletes had no idea that what they were taking would affect both their general health and their fertility in the years to come. In 1998 East German coaches and doctors began to be put on trial for their crimes, and the former chief doctor of the national swimming federation was convicted of causing bodily harm to no fewer than 59 swimmers.

America had its own scandal in 2005, when Victor Conte admitted in court that, through his Burlinghame Bay Area Laboratory Co-Operative, he had run a doping 'ring' which involved dozens of athletes. One of them was the sprinter Marion Jones, who later admitted taking the steroid THG and was stripped of her five Olympic medals.

But an even more sensational fall from grace had occurred a few years before – in 1988 at Seoul. It was then that the popular Jamaican-born Canadian sprinter Ben Johnson had streaked ahead of his great rival Carl Lewis in the 100 metres to take gold in a new world record time of 9.79 secs.

Too good to be true? Alas yes, because although Johnson at first denied the evidence of the tests taken immediately after the race, his doctor eventually admitted the truth. Look away if you're squeamish, but Johnson had been given an injection of a steroid used to fatten cattle before they're taken to market.

A RACE TOO FAR

For the Japanese runner Kokichi Tsuburaya Olympic failure was too much to bear. He had picked up a bronze in the 1964 marathon and hoped to do even better four years later, not only training with increased rigour but giving up his fiancée, too.

Unhappily he sustained two injuries in the year before the 1968 Games, and it soon became clear to him that he couldn't get back to full fitness in time.

Believing that he had let his country down, Tsuburaya slit his wrists with a razor blade. He was found clutching his bronze medal, having written a farewell note: 'Can't run any more.'

THAT'S NO LADY . . .

Question: When is a woman Olympic athlete not a woman athlete?

Answer: Either when she's so illegally pumped up with steroids and hormones that she develops male characteristics – or when she actually is a man in disguise.

Gender testing began at the Tokyo Oympics in 1964, but there were suspicions about some of the more masculine entrants in the women's events well before then.

Dora Ratjen

Her deep voice was unusual, but didn't her refusal to share the showers with other female athletes offer even more of a clue? Ratjen, who competed in the high jump for Germany in the 1936 Olympics and took fourth place, was finally unmasked two years later when, noticing her marked 'five o'clock shadow', a railway conductor reported to the police 'a man dressed as a woman' – a much more shocking spectacle in those days, of course.

A doctor was called and the (slightly complicated) truth was revealed. The athlete had been born with a defect which led the midwife to declare the baby a girl. Later medical opinion, however, was that she certainly wasn't. Once all the fuss was over, Dora became Heinrich and disappeared from the athletics limelight.

Stanisława Walasiewicz

At the Berlin Olympics the Polish sprinter was hoping to repeat her 1932 victory in the 100 metres. When she was beaten into second place by Helen Stephens of the USA, she declared that her opponent was a man – and Stephens had to undergo a test to prove that she wasn't.

What a nerve! Walasiewicz later moved to America, where she ran under the name Stella Walsh. In December 1980, now 69, she was innocently caught up in an armed robbery and shot dead. The autopsy showed that she had all the trappings of a man. As with Ratjen, the case wasn't completely straightforward. It was revealed that she had both an XX and an XY pair of chromosomes – highlighting the genuine difficulties the authorities often experience in coming to a fair ruling on gender issues.

Tamara and Irina Press

Built like Russian tanks, with huge muscles and prominent jaws, the brawny Press sisters set more than twenty world track and field records during the 1960s, and won five golds between them during the 1960 and 1964 Olympics – Tamara in the shot put and discus, her younger sister in the 80 metres hurdles and the pentathlon.

The doubters called them 'the Press brothers', but we shall probably never know whether they were in fact male or whether (the Soviets of course denied it) their outwardly masculine characteristics were created by chemical means. All we can say is that they retired as soon as gender testing was introduced – officially to look after their sick mother.

PULLING A FAST ONE

Dirty tricks and their shaming exposure litter the story of the Olympic Games. Here are a few sorry examples from a variety of disciplines.

• At Montreal in 1976 the British pentathlon fencing team were dumbfounded when the Russian Boris Onishenko beat two of their team in succession without seeming to have landed his épée on either. The blades were attached to wires which triggered a buzzer on the judges' table when there was a hit, and on the second occasion the losing Briton, Jim Fox, lodged an appeal, thinking that there must be a short-circuit in the system.

He never for a moment suspected Onishenko, who was a Red Army major, one of the world's top pentathletes and a winner of an invidividual silver medal at the previous Games.

The Russians attempted to swap the suspect épée for another, but the suspicious judges insisted that it be properly tested – and then it emerged that it had been fitted with a hidden push-button circuit breaker which allowed Onishenko to claim a hit whenever he wished.

• The Puerto Rican athlete Madeline de Jesus injured herself while taking part in the 1984 long jump, and she knew she couldn't possibly put up a decent show in the heats of the 4 x 400-metre relay. Help was at hand, though: her identical twin Margaret was in Los Angeles to watch, so she quietly took her sister's place in the line-up.

Margaret was obviously no slouch, because the team made it through to the final, but when the Puerto Rican coach discovered their secret he withdrew the team from the event.

• Special dispensations apart, you can only take part in the Olympics if you achieve the set qualifying time for your event. The Hungarian swimming team had a problem before the Atlanta Games in 1996 because, thanks to an administrative blunder, half of its 22 members hadn't had their times officially recorded. Their national federation came up with a neat solution to that little problem: they invented a fictitious pre-Olympic event at which not only

'TIMID PUSSYFOOTERS'

The American swimmer Lance Larson seemed to come home fractionally ahead of his Australian rival John Devitt in the 100 metres freestyle at Rome in 1960, and both men were amazed when the judges gave Devitt the gold.

The evidence of six stopwatches and an unofficial electronic timer was ignored, and the Americans, not surprisingly, were furious.

The treasurer of the US Olympic Committee, Max Ritter, described the judges in decidedly unOlympian terms as 'a bunch of timid, unemployed pussyfooters'. He called for machines to be used in future – and they were.

were imaginary times entered (obviously), but two swimmers were disqualified to provide an authentic touch.

Hungary duly picked up six medals – among them the 200-metres gold for Attila Czene, who was one of those with a 'phantom' time – but when the story came out, the head of the federation, Tamas Gyarfas, resigned.

- At Athens in 2004 the Greek sprinters

Kostas Kenteris and Katerina Thanous failed to turn up for a drugs test. What on earth had happened to them? Ah, they'd been involved in a motorbike accident and had been taken to hospital suffering from cuts and bruises.

There were a few oddities in their story, however. To begin with, there were no witnesses to the accident. Secondly, the driver who had supposedly taken them to hospital was equally elusive. Thirdly, when they emerged from their ordeal a few days later to announce their withdrawal from the Games they showed not a trace of their injuries.

Eventually they admitted failing three recent doping tests, and they were given a two-year ban from all competitions.

• And what if you can't even trust the judges? Insiders watched with astonishment at Seoul in 1988 as the decidedly average local boxer Park Si-hun proceeded from one controversial bout to another on his way to Olympic light-middleweight gold.

His early victory over the Sudan's Abdallah

Ramadan was won through a series of kidney punches which the referee declined to punish, and the Sudanese were so incensed that when one of their super-heavyweights was matched against another South Korean they protested by throwing in the towel before the fight had even begun.

In the final Park was completely outclassed by the young American Roy Jones – later voted the outstanding boxer at the games – who landed 86 punches to the South Korean's 32 and put him down on the canvas for a mandatory count in the second round. That didn't prevent the judges giving the gold to Park on a 3–2 majority.

It can't have been much consolation to Jones that a sheepish Park raised his opponent's arm on the victory stand, that two of the judges were subsequently banned for life or that, because of this farce, the Olympic rules were changed to take account of the number of punches landed.

Referring to this fight and a number like it, Boxing News described Seoul as 'the Games of Shame'. But what was behind the fix? Some thought the judges were simply doing their best to please the host nation. Cynics, of course, suggested that cash had changed hands – although this was never proved.

MONEY TALKS

But can anyone doubt that the huge amount of money swilling about the Olympic circus encourages the unscrupulous to take advantage? The 1984 Los Angeles Olympics began the lurch from a comparatively low-key event to a multi-million dollar extravanza in which private corporations bid for specific marketing privileges to secure bulging coffers for themselves, the host city and the IOC.

Athens managed to make a loss in 2004, but every other Games since Los Angeles has made at least a tidy profit, and at times an astronomical one. Take a look at the IOC's income from the 2008 Olympics in Beijing. Its gross revenue amounted to some $2.4 billion, including $1.73 billion from broadcasting rights and $436 million from sponsorship and marketing. Its net profits came to a cool $383 million, and its reserve funds in 2009 were all of $466 million.

When the 'think tank' One World Trust assessed thirty international bodies in 2008 it found that the IOC was the least accountable of them all, with the president and the executive board having several key powers unchecked by the organisation as a whole.

THE OLYMPIC RINGS

Pierre de Coubertin devised the Olympic emblem of five interlocking rings (blue, yellow, black, green and red) to symbolise 'the five parts of the world won over to Olympism'.

The rings are reckoned by copyright lawyers to be the most heavily protected image in the world. After all, the IOC makes a huge amount of money from officially approved merchandise.

We'd be in big trouble for printing them on their own, so you'll just have to imagine you can see them – right here ⟶

We've already mentioned the scandal over IOC members being bribed to vote for cities keen to host the Olympics (page 71). The IOC,

recognising that this corruption had taken hold in the summer event as well as the winter one, introduced strict new rules forbidding members to visit the bid cities.

But there are plenty of other people keen to sink their fingers into this lucrative pie. Keeping the Games clean is a perpetual headache, and sometimes you're tempted to wonder who they're really for.

Mercifully, however – despite all the financial shenanigans, the nationalistic fervour, the dirty tricks and the bad blood – the Olympics have been redeemed time and again by athletic performances of the utmost grace, power and endurance . . .

beep!

SPECIAL OLYMPICS

Two indomitable American women were the chief inspiration behind the Special Olympics (motto: 'Let me win. But if I cannot win, let me be brave in the attempt') – the international organisation for people with intellectual disabilities.

In 1968 Anne McGlone Burke, a PE teacher in Chicago, launched an Olympic-style competition for athletes with special needs, and she approached Eunice Kennedy Shriver, head of the Joseph P. Kennedy Jr Foundation, for funding. Shriver had already formed a day camp for children with intellectual disabilities, and between them these two influential women (Burke later became a Supreme Court judge) developed an event which was officially recognised by the IOC in 1988.

Today Special Olympics are held every two years, alternating between the main summer and winter Games, but there are many other events, too – there are currently around three million athletes of all ages who take part in training and competitions in more than 180 countries.

It's estimated that about three per cent of the global population (that's 200 million people) have intellectual disabilities, and Special Olympics sets out not only to provide them with uplifting sports events but to offer various kinds of help – including free health screenings in the world's most neglected populations – in an attempt to make the subject better understood and free from stigma.

Here are a few achievements, quoted from the Special Olympics' own website, which claims that it is now 'the fastest-growing volunteer movement on the planet':

- In Afghanistan, the 2009 Special Olympics World Winter Games floor hockey team was honoured with congratulations from the highest levels of government as a tribute to their success.

- In Romania, children who were solitary and forgotten now participate in sports training and interact regularly with the community outside their institutions.

- In the United States, the young girl who was bullied or isolated is chosen as 'homecoming queen'.

- In China, people who were hidden away in their homes now receive vocational and literacy training at thousands of Sunshine Centres across the provinces.

**BOB
BEAMON**

**DAWN
FRASER**

MUHAMMAD ALI

USAIN BOLT

**FANNY
BLANKERS-
KOEN**

PAAVO NURMI

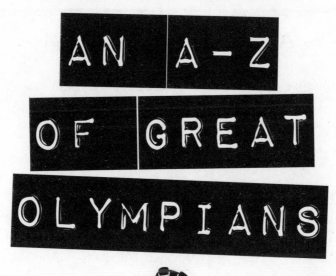

Although enthusiasts will always argue about which athletes demand to appear on a list of all-time Olympic greats, this chapter boldly selects twenty of the best for inclusion in the Very Peculiar History pantheon.

It's impossible for the list to embrace every discipline and every country, but all of these stars have won gold, none has been banned for drug abuse and our feeling is that Zeus himself would look down upon their achievements with admiration.

AGAINST THE ODDS I

We've already featured George Eyser (page 53) who won gold despite having only one leg. He wasn't the only athlete to overcome heavy odds in order to become an Olympic champion:

- **Ray Lewry** contracted polio when he was a child in Indiana. He spent some time in a wheelchair, and it was feared he might never walk again. The American later showed admirable 'can-do' spirit in devising his own strengthening exercises, and between 1900 and 1908 he won a clutch of golds at the standing jump events.

- The American marksman **Sidney Hinds** was competing in the 1924 free rifle team event in Paris when a disgruntled Belgian competitor flung his loaded weapon to the ground and a bullet lodged in Hinds's foot. He shrugged this handicap aside by scoring a perfect 50 in the final, and his team picked up the gold.

- **Richard Norris Williams,** who partnered his fellow American Hazel Wightman to victory in the mixed tennis doubles at the same Games, was very lucky to be there. He'd been a passenger on the **Titanic** when she foundered in 1912, and most of those who clambered onto a half-submerged collapsible boat with him died of exposure.

Muhammad Ali

He won the light heavyweight championship in Rome in 1960 fighting under what he would later call his 'slave name' of Cassius Clay. That's still how he was known just under four years later, when (having turned professional) he won the world heavyweight championship by defeating the seemingly impregnable Sonny Liston.

Three further years on and he had converted to Islam, changing his name to Muhammad Ali, and he further outraged many of his fellow countrymen by refusing to fight in the Vietnam war. Today, however, he's a national treasure, and in 1996, visibly suffering from Parkinson's disease, he was chosen to light the Olympic flame at the Atlanta Games.

Bob Beamon

After Beamon had shattered the world long jump record at Mexico City in 1968, the defending champion – Lynn Davies of Great Britain – admiringly told the American that he had 'destroyed this event', while the sports journalist Dick Schaap went on to write a book about it called *The Perfect Jump*.

Beamon didn't at first realise how prodigious his leap had been, because it was announced in metres, and he sank to his knees and covered his face in shock when he realised that at 8.9 m (29 ft 2 in) it was all of 55 cm (21¾ in) further than anyone had ever jumped before.

It's true that he was helped by the high altitude and a following wind, but Beamon's distance remains to this day the best ever achieved at the Olympics.

Adebe Bikila

We've already celebrated (*pages 87–89*) Bikila becoming the first African to win the Olympic marathon. Four years later, in 1964, he went one better, being the first athlete to win the competition twice.

His double was all the more remarkable because forty days before the Tokyo Games he collapsed with acute appendicitis. Although he began jogging exercises in the hospital courtyard at night he wasn't expected to be fit enough to take part in the marathon – but he won it in a new record time.

OLYMPIC BESTS

LONG JUMP

Men:
Bob Beamon (USA)
8.90m   1968 Mexico City

Women:
Jackie Joyner-Kersee (USA)
7.40m   1988 Seoul

Fanny Blankers-Koen
The Dutch runner not only had her career interrupted by the Second World War, but she came to the 1948 London Games at the age of thirty soon after having given birth to two children and now pregnant with a third.

The manager of the British athletics team said she was 'too old to make the grade', but The Flying Housewife – as she became known – proved him wrong in dramatic style. With victories in the 100 metres, 200 metres, the 80 metres hurdles and the 4x100 metres relay, she became the first woman to win four Olympic golds and the first to win four in a single Games. In 1999, at a gala run by the International Association

OLYMPIC BESTS

100 metres

Men:
Usain Bolt (Jamaica)
9.63   2012 London

Women:
Florence Griffith-Joyner (USA)
10.62   1988 Seoul

200 metres

Men:
Usain Bolt (Jamaica)
19.30   2008 Beijing

Women:
Florence Griffith-Joyner (USA)
21.34   1988 Seoul

400 metres

Men:
Michael Johnson (USA)
43.49   1996 Atlanta

Women:
Marie-José Pérec (France)
48.25   1996 Atlanta

of Athletics Federations, she was nominated Female Athlete of the Century.

Usain Bolt

His surname was made for the headline writers, and he didn't let them down at the Beijing Games in 2008 and the London games in 2012. Already accustomed to breaking world records, he won the 100m, 200m and, with his Jamaican teammates, the 4x100m relay at both games. At the 2012 Summer Olympics in London he became the first man in history to defend both the 100m and 200m Olympic sprint titles.

Seb Coe

The British runner had some wonderful tussles during the 1980s with his fellow countrymen Steve Ovett and Steve Cram. For precisely one hour in 1980 (until Ovett set a new time for the mile) he held all four of the classic middle-distance world records – the 800m, 1000m, 1500m and the mile. Nobody had done that before and nobody has repeated the achievement since.

Coe suffered a huge disappointment in losing

to Ovett in the 800m in Moscow that year, but he responded gutsily to win the 1500m. It was a case of *déjà vu* in Los Angeles in 1984, with silver in the 800m and gold in the 1500m. Coe, by now a life peer, led London's bid to stage the 2012 Olympics in the city, and became chairman of the organising committee.

SEB COE BEATS STEVE OVETT IN THE 1980 OLYMPICS 1500M.

Nadia Comaneci

Gymnasts have to be 16 years old to take part in the Olympics these days, but this Romanian girl was just 14 when she won three golds at Montreal in 1976. Her brilliance was too much for the judges' machines, which weren't calibrated to allow for marks of 10. They had to post marks of 1.0 – but nobody was left in any doubt what that signified.

AGAINST THE ODDS 2

• The 16-year-old **Betty Robinson** became the first woman to win an Olympic track event when she took gold in the 100 metres at Amsterdam in 1928, but her appearance in the Berlin Games eight years later was more remarkable still.

In 1931 she was so badly injured in a plane crash that the man who found her thought she was dead and drove her to the local mortuary. Unconscious for seven weeks, with multiple injuries to her arms and legs, she later spent six months in a wheelchair and a further nine on crutches. After two years she could walk, but she was unable to bend her legs fully at the knee, making it impossible to begin a sprint event. Undaunted, she switched to relays – and won gold as part of the US 4x100 metres team.

• **Tommy Green** had rickets as a child and was unable to walk until he was five. As if that wasn't bad enough, he was later the victim of a gas attack while serving in the British Army during the First World War, and was sent home with damaged lungs.

He took up race walking in his early thirties, winning the first event he entered. In 1932, under a scorching Californian sun, he won gold in the 50km walk – coming in more than seven minutes ahead of his nearest rival.

ATHLETES ON CELLULOID

Apart from Leni Riefenstahl's *Olympia* (page 102), the best-known film based on the Games is *Chariots of Fire*, which tells the story – in parts fictitiously – of the British runners Harold Abrahams and Eric Liddell at the 1924 Olympics.

Some Olympic athletes have themselves gone on to appear in films. During the Depresssion, when his sporting career was over, the great **Jim Thorpe** (page 62) drifted from job to job. He played Indian chiefs and other 'extras' in Hollywood, and can be seen as one of the dancers in *King Kong*.

Harold Sakata of the USA, who won silver in the light heavyweight weightlifting event in 1948, took up professional wrestling before becoming an actor. His most celebrated role was the frighteningly vicious Oddjob in the James Bond film *Goldfinger*.

But the most famous of all the 'athlete stars' was the US swimmer **Johnny Weissmuller**, who won five golds and a bronze at the 1924 and 1928 Olympics. Born in Germany, he had contracted polio as a child and took up swimming to strengthen his body. (He might have appeared in one of our Against the Odds boxes.) That body was eventually so impressive that he was chosen to play the lead role in no fewer than a dozen Tarzan films. Once heard, that yodelling cry is unforgettable!

OLYMPIC BESTS

HIGH JUMP

Men:
Charles Austin (USA)
2.39 m   1996 Atlanta

Women:
Yelena Slesarenko (Russia)
2.06 m   2004 Athens

POLE VAULT

Men:
Renaud Lavillenie (France)
5.97 m   2012 London

Women:
Yelena Isinbayeva (Russia)
5.05 m   2008 Beijing

TRIPLE JUMP

Men:
Kenny Harrison (USA)
18.09 m   1996 Atlanta

Women:
Françoise Mbango Etone (Cameroon)
15.39 m   2008 Beijing

Dick Fosbury

Not many sportsmen have a manoeuvre named after them, but here's the man who gave us the 'Fosbury flop'. The American was never happy with the standard high-jump technique of leaping over the bar face down, so he invented his own method of going over backwards. He gradually refined it – ignoring the predictable jokes at his expense – until he burst onto the Olympic scene in Mexico City in 1968 by taking the gold medal and setting a new record. Quirky? Well, within a few years nearly all the top high jumpers were following suit!

Dawn Fraser

This Australian swimmer won eight Olympic medals, including four golds, and was the first to win individual golds for the same event in three consecutive Games – the 100m freestyle in 1956, 1960 and 1964.

She fell out with her commercially minded swimming union in 1964 for wearing an old, more comfortable costume rather than the one supplied by the sponsors. (There can be few greater sins in the modern Games.) She was then arrested for 'stealing' an Olympic flag from outside Emperor Hirohito's palace: although she wasn't charged, and the emperor gave her the flag as a souvenir, her union promptly suspended her for ten years. The ban was lifted too late for her to train for the following Games.

Michael Johnson

The American sprinter turned up for his 1996 races in Atlanta wearing gold-coloured boots, but these nonetheless earned him less publicity than becoming the first athlete to win both the 200m and the 400m in the same Olympics. When he successfully defended his 400m title

OLYMPIC BESTS

Decathlon

(Men only)

Roman Sebrie (Czech Republic)
8893 points   2004 Athens

Heptathlon

(Women only)

Jackie Joyner-Kersee (United States)
7291 points   1988 Seoul

four years later in Sydney (at the ripe old age of 32) he earned himself a special record – as the oldest ever gold medallist in an Olympic track event shorter than 5000m.

Jackie Joyner-Kersee

The American began as a basketball star, but her athletic all-roundness is demonstrated by the fact that three of her Olympic medals (silver in 1984 and gold in 1988 and 1992) were won in that toughest of events, the heptathlon – two consecutive days of competition, embracing the 100m hurdles, the high jump, the shot put, the 200m run, the long jump, the javelin and the 800m.

A world record holder in the long jump, she was voted Greatest Female Athlete of the 20th Century by *Sports Illustrated for Women* magazine, ahead of 'Babe' Didrikson (*page 58*).

'Kip' Keino

Kipchoge Keino was the forerunner of a long line of Kenyan middle and long distance athletes, first making an impact on the Olympics in unlikely fashion. He came to Mexico City in 1968 suffering violent pains

AGAINST THE ODDS 3

- In 1938, while serving as a sergeant in the army, the Hungarian marksman **Károly Takács** had his pistol hand completely shattered by a faulty grenade. His promising shooting career seemed to be over – until he roused himself from despair and taught himself to use his left hand instead.

  At the 1948 Games the favourite in the rapid-fire pistol event, Diaz Saenz Valiente, asked him what he was doing in London, and he replied that he was there to learn. At the medals ceremony, after Takács had broken the world record to take gold, the Argentinian told him, 'You have learned enough!'

- No prospective athlete could have had a much tougher start in life than the black American **Wilma Rudolph**. She was born prematurely, suffered infantile paralysis (she had to wear a brace on her twisted left leg and foot) and then picked up scarlet fever, chickenpox, whooping cough and measles. Not until she was 12 had her leg straightened sufficienty to dispense with the brace – and yet by the age of 16 she was a member of the US track and field team and won bronze in the 4x100 metre relay at the 1956 Melbourne Games.

  At the 1960 Rome Olympics she won gold in the 100 metres, 200 metres and 4x100 metres relay, by which time she was regarded as the fastest woman in the world.

brought on by a gall bladder infection, but he was determined to take part in the 10,000m, the 5000m and the 1500m – in that order.

He was among the leaders two laps from home in the first race when he collapsed in pain, but he recovered to join the start of the 5000m four days later and took the silver. Perhaps the 1500m seemed easy by comparison, but

OLYMPIC BESTS

800 METRES

Men:
David Rudisha (Kenya)
1.40.91   2012 London

Women:
Nadezhda Olizarenko (Soviet Union)
1.53.43   1980 Moscow

1500 METRES

Men:
Noah Ngeny (Kenya)
3.32.07   2000 Sydney

Women:
Paula Ivan (Romania)
3.53.96m   1988 Seoul

poor Keino had to jog to the stadium when he was caught in a traffic jam, and he knew that the only way to beat the American Jim Ryun – known for his devastating 'kick' at the end of a race – was to set a very fast pace and keep to it. He took gold by the largest margin in the event's history – and when his wife gave birth that same day back in Kenya, the baby girl was proudly named Milka Olympia Chelagat. Four years later, emphasising his versatility, Keino won the 3000m steeplechase and came second in the 1500m.

Olga Korbut
With ten out of ten for charm, little Olga won everyone's heart at the 1972 Munich Games – especially when she wept upon messing up her uneven bars routine. She didn't mess up much else, though, taking three golds and a silver, and one of her moves (known as the Korbut flip) is still used by gymnasts today.

Carl Lewis
At Los Angeles in 1984 the American athlete set out to equal the great Jesse Owens's feat of winning four golds at a single Olympics – in the long jump, the 100m, the 200m and the

OLYMPIC BESTS

SHOT PUT

Men:
Ulf Timmermann (East Germany)
22.47 m   1998 Seoul

Women:
Ilona Slupianek (East Germany)
22.41 m   1980 Moscow

DISCUS

Men:
Virgilijus Alekna (Lithuania)
69.89 m   2004 Athens

Women:
Martina Hellmann (East Germany)
72.30 m   1988 Seoul

HAMMER THROW

Men:
Sergey Litvinov (Soviet Union)
84.80 m   1988 Seoul

Women:
Tatyana Lysenko (Russia)
78.18 m   2012 London

sprint relay. Careful to pace himself, once he had posted an impressive distance in the long jump early on he chose to abandon his last four attempts. This tactic worked – he went on to win all four events – but some spectators had been hoping that he would go for a new world record, and they booed him.

When Lewis's father died the year before the next Olympics, the athlete put his 100m gold medal in his hand to lie in the coffin with him, assuring his mother that he would win another one. At Seoul in 1988 this seemed mere wishful thinking, as Ben Johnson streaked away to win, but Johnson (*page 128*) was found to have taken drugs, and Lewis got his gold after all. He won nine Olympic golds in all, the last

OLYMPIC BESTS

JAVELIN

Men:
Andreas Thorkildsen (Norway)
90.57 m   2008 Beijing

Women:
Osleidys Menéndez (Cuba)
71.53 m   2004 Athens

of them when he won the long jump for a remarkable fourth time in 1996. No wonder that, three years later, the IOC voted him Sportsman of the Century.

Paavo Nurmi

Those of us who find a slow trot around a 400m course exhausting can only wonder at the achievements of the Flying Finn, who between 1920 and 1928 won Olympic gold at 1500m, 5000m, 10,000m, the cross country (*page 88*) and the steeplechase. Even more astounding, perhaps, is the fact that he would often run two long-distance races with only a short break in between.

Jesse Owens

A mixture of supreme talent and political impact (*page 104*) have elevated Owens to the very front of the Olympic pack. We'll add here only that in the year before Hitler's Berlin Games he set six world records in a single day.

GREAT LOSERS

You don't have to be a champion to win the admiration of an Olympic audience – as witness the ludicrously brave leaps of the incompetent English ski-jumper 'Eddie the Eagle' at the 1988 Winter Olympics.

The summer equivalents were the dogged performances of two swimmers from Equatorial Guinea, Paula Barila Bolopa ('Paula the Crawler') and Eric Moussambania ('Eric the Eel').

Both were allowed to compete in the heats of the 2000 Sydney Games despite not having posted the required qualifying times. That was because their training conditions were so poor at home that neither had ever swum in a proper competition pool (they used a local hotel when the guests weren't about, and otherwise swam in the sea where sharks were an ever-present danger).

Eric turned up for his race in baggy blue shorts with the draw-strings dangling, and faced competition from two body-suited, but similarly inexperienced, swimmers from Niger and Tajikistan. Fortunately for him they both toppled into the water before the gun had sounded, and so were disqualified for having made false starts.

All alone, Eric set off to complete two laps of the 50-metre pool – if he could. Lifeguards stood by as he splashed ever more slowly through the water, completely exhausted. His time, when he at last finished, was several seconds slower than the record for double the distance.

And after those heroics? He may have won, but Eric's time was too slow to take him forward to the next round.

Paula, 'racing' three days later, had only 50 metres to swim, but she still came in (last) nearly 40 seconds behind the winner. Even diving into the water from the starting blocks had been difficult for her, explained her trainer – not only because it was a new experience, but because she had a fear of heights and it was a long way down to the water.

Michael Phelps

Swimming aficionados will never cease debating whether Phelps or Mark Spitz was the greatest ever swimmer, but we give the vote to Phelps on his medal tally. Phelps, who won six first places and two thirds in 2004, topped this with an incredible eight golds at Beijing four years later, and a further four golds and two silvers at the 2012 games.

OLYMPIC BESTS

100M HURDLES

Men:
Liu Xiang (China)
12.91 secs   2004 Athens

Women:
Joanna Hayes (USA)
12.37 secs   2004 Athens

400M HURDLES

Men:
Kevin Young (USA)
46.78 secs   1992 Barcelona

Women:
Melaine Walker (Jamaica)
52.64 secs   2008 Beijing

AGAINST THE ODDS 4

- Motherhood can be tricky for athletes, but **Valerie Brisco-Hooks** made it especially difficult for herself by dropping physical exercise altogether for nine months either side of her son Alvin's birth in 1982. In fact she led a pretty unhealthy lifestyle, and at one time weighed more than 14 stone (900 kg), against her running weight of around 9 stone (590kg). She hadn't left it too late, though. In 1984 she became the first athlete to win both the 200 metres and 400 metres in a single Games, and she also took gold with the US team in the 4x400 metres.

- **Greg Louganis** is regarded as the greatest diver of all time, but he had a lot to overcome at the 1988 Olympics in Seoul. During a qualifying round he was executing a reverse two-and-a-half somersault pike when he hit the back of his head on the diving board and fell awkwardly into the water.

What the medics who stitched his scalp wound didn't know was that their patient was HIV positive. Louganis knew it, and he worried about the possibility of spreading his condition to other divers if he had bled in the pool. (He hadn't.) He also had to cope with the fear that he might hit the board again – but he overcame his demons to win double diving gold for the second Games in succession.

Steve Redgrave

Rowers don't get much of a look-in when it comes to 'hall of fame'-type lists, but the UK's Steve Redgrave has earned his place by winning his fifth successive gold at Sydney in 2000 – this time in the coxless fours – becoming only the fourth athlete anywhere to have achieved the feat.

Mind you, it might never have happened. Interviewed straight after the 1996 event, an exhausted Redgrave said anyone finding him near a rowing boat again should shoot him!

Lasse Viren

Another great long-distance Finnish runner, he seemed to save his best performances for the Olympic Games. He won the 5,000m/ 10,000m double in both 1972 and 1976, with devastating late bursts of speed. The first of his 10,000m wins was the more remarkable because he took a fall during the 12th lap, yet ended up winning in a world record time.

OLYMPIC BESTS

5,000 metre

Men:
Kenenisa Bekele (Ethiopia)
12:57.82   2008 Beijing

Women:
Gabriela Szabo (Romania)
14:40.79   2000 Sydney

10,000 metres

Men:
Kenenisa Bekele (Ethiopia)
27:01.17   2008 Beijing

Women:
Tirunesh Dibaba (Ethiopia)
29:54.66   2008 Beijing

3,000 metres steeplechase

Men:
Julius Kariuki (Kenya)
8:05.51   1988 Seoul

Women:
Gulnara Galkina-Samitova (Russia)
8:58.81   2008 Beijing

Emil Zátopek

After the Czech won both the 5,000m and 10,000m at the 1956 Helsinki Games – he'd taken silver and gold, respectively, four years earlier – he made a last-minute decision to have a go at the marathon. He'd never run that distance before, but (as you've probably already guessed) he won that, too. Oh, and he set new Olympic records in all three races.

After about 15 km (9 miles) of the marathon Zátopek found himself alongside the British world record holder, Jim Peters, and casually asked him what he made of the race so far. Peters, who was in fact finding it very hard going, thought he'd score a psychological advantage by replying that the pace was too slow – to which the Czech responded by accelerating away into the distance.

Zátopek often looked distressed while he ran, pulling faces and even panting and wheezing, but he had a simple explanation for this: 'I wasn't talented enough to run and smile at the same time,' he said.

LONDON'S HAT-TRICK

Five cities threw their hats into the ring to stage the 2012 Olympic Games, and there was a heart-stopping moment in July 2005 when (with Moscow, New York and Madrid already eliminated) the people of London and Paris massed in their public squares to hear the result of the IOC's secret electronic ballot in Singapore.

London won the nomination by just 54 votes to 50, so becoming the first city to be awarded the Games for a third time. Alas, the jubilation on the streets would all too soon give way to a mood of sober reflection.

WHAT HAPPENED BEFORE

London's bid chairman, Lord (formerly Seb) Coe, was ecstatic, promising the Games would prove 'magic happens' and would inspire young people around the world. If he knew his Olympic history he would certainly have hoped for a better showing than London had managed in the past.

1908

The first time the city hosted the Games it had to arrange things in a bit of a hurry. Rome was meant to be the venue, but Vesuvius erupted in 1906 and the Italians had other claims on their money.

One of the strangest decisions was giving the marathon's catering contract to the meat extract company Oxo, which provided refreshments along the route – not only bananas, raisins and milk, but rice pudding, hot and cold Oxo and 'Oxo and soda'. Ugh!

What let these Games down, though, wasn't its organisation but some serial outbreaks of national pride.

Sven wondered whether the rice pudding had been a bit of a handicap.

- Several Irish athletes refused to take part because they wanted to represent their own country rather than a Great Britain team.
- These were the first Olympics in which the athletes marched with their national flags, and Finland – then under Russian rule – chose to march with no flag at all rather than under the Russian one.
- During the opening ceremony the US flag-bearer refused to 'dip' it to the royal box, explaining later that 'this flag dips to no earthly king'.
- This led to ill-feeling between the British and American camps, which spilled over not only into the 400m (*page 117*), but the tug-of-war as well. After the British team, from Liverpool Police, had won a swift victory, their opponents accused them of wearing illegal boots with steel spikes and heels. (Not guilty, m'lud: they were regulation police boots.)

1948

Held so soon after the Second World War was over (Germany and Japan weren't invited and the Soviet Union declined), these were the austerity Games.

With food and clothing severely rationed in Britain, visiting athletes were expected to bring their own grub with them.
Wembley Stadium had survived the bombing,

but no new facilities were built. The 'Olympic village' for male competitors was an army camp in Uxbridge, while the women were put up in dormitories at Southlands College.

The Games were televised for the first time, which would have been more of a landmark had more than a handful of people owned a TV set in those days.

Although 4,000 athletes took part, this surely has to take the prize for being most drab event in the history of the Olympics. You might even call it 'Spartan' . . .

WHAT HAPPENED NEXT

What happened immediately after London won its Olympic bid in 2005 – the very next day in fact – was that a series of terrorist bombs on the underground system and a bus killed 52 people and wounded hundreds more.

This outrage had no connection with the Games, but it served to remind the city of how vulnerable it would be to attack in 2012.
Such an atrocity apart, London's third

WHAT THEY'LL BE PLAYING

Alongside the track and field events, there will be 28 different sports at the 2016 Rio Olympics:

Aquatics	Handball
Archery	Judo
Athletics	Modern Pentathlon
Badminton	Rowing
Basketball	Rugby Sevens
Boxing	Sailing
Canoe / kayak	Shooting
Cycling	Table Tennis
Equestrian	Taekwondo
Fencing	Tennis
Field Hockey	Triathlon
Football	Volleyball
Golf	Weightlifting
Gymnastics	Wrestling

Olympics was bound to be more illustrious than its two forerunners, wasn't it? Not a doubt of it – and yet in October 2008, with preparations not yet at the half-way stage, the Games were dealt the horrible blow of a world-wide banking crisis which threatened economic melt-down.

Did those defeated Paris Olympic bidders suddenly thank their lucky stars?

The Olympics certainly couldn't escape the tremors that rumbled in the wake of this financial earthquake, and some cuts had to be made to a budget which had already grown from an original estimate of £2.4bn to a staggering £9.3bn. This sum included:

- New venues, including an Olympic Park at Stratford and the Athletes' Village: **£3.1bn**
- Regeneration and infrastructure: **£1.7bn**
- Extra security: **£600m**
- Tax: **£840m**
- Paralympics, community sport etc: **£390m**
- A 'contingency sum' in case costs should rise even further (surely not!): **£2.7bn**

You won't be surprised to learn that some critics condemned this outlay as indecently vast for a brief sporting event which might glorify London but would have few benefits for the people of Britain as a whole.

They also accused the government of tearing up large tracts of working class east London (that 'regeneration and infrastructure') in order to build sports facilities which would have no long-term value – especially for the people whose homes and businesses had been removed to make way for them.

The government's reply to this carping was, of course, defiantly upbeat. It would provide £6bn towards the costs itself, with further funds coming from the National Lottery and from London council tax payers – who had to cough up an extra £20 a year per household for the privilege of having the Games on their doorstep. Other income would come from:

- TV and marketing deals: **£560m**
- Sponsorship and official suppliers: **£450m**
- Ticket revenues: **£300m**
- Licensing: **£60m**
- The London Development Agency: **£250m**

MEET THE MASCOTS

Vinicius and Tom are the child-friendly mascots for the 2016 Games. Vinicius has mammalian traits and represents Brazilian wildlife. Tom has a head of leaves and symbolizes the vegetation of Brazilian rainforests.

Here's a list of all the previous mascots:

1972 Munich: Waldi, a dachshund
1976 Montreal: Amik, a beaver
1980 Moscow: Misha, a bear
1984 Los Angeles: Sam, an eagle
1988 Seoul: Hodori, a tiger
1992 Barcelona: Cobi, a dog
1996 Atlanta: Izzy, a computerised fantasy
    figure
2000 Sydney: Syd, a platypus; Olly, a
    kookaburra; and Millie, an echidna
2004 Athens: Athena and Phevos, based on
    dolls found at archaeological sites in Greece
2008 Beijing: Five little creatures collectively
    called Fuwa, whose names put together said
    'Welcome to Beijing!'
2012 London: Two strange one-eyed creatures
    named Wenlock (page 40) and Mandeville
    (page 98).

And then there were the long-term effects, officially known as 'the legacy'. These would include the expansion of Stratford Regional Station and improvements to the many rail services which used it, together with a range of other spin-offs:

- The Olympic Village's polyclinic would be converted into a life-long learning centre for the east London community.

- The Village would be converted into 3,600 apartments, most of them affordable housing.

- The media and press centre would become a 'creative industries' centre for east London.

- Four arenas would be dismantled after the Games and relocated in other parts of the UK, along with the water polo and 50m training pools.

- Sports equipment used in the Games would be given to charities.

THE BIGGEST PRIZE

And so the clock ticked away towards July 27th, 2012, and the Games of the XXX Olympiad. 'We're taking home the biggest prize in sport,' Lord Coe had said when London won the bid, and he'd worked tirelessly ever since to justify that infectious optimism. He'd also been determined to keep sport at the forefront, despite the thousand and one distractions that, as ever, threatened to get in the way of it.

'I'm a former competitor,' he replied, asked whether athletes might have to perform at times which suited the television companies. 'I have the instincts of a competitor, and I know when a schedule works for competitors and when it doesn't. Are we going to be seeing the 100 metres at 2am? The answer is categorically "no".'

So a fine, athlete-centred Olympics, then, with all the commercialism, national fervour, doping scandals and back-biting relegated to the shadows? The waiting world held its breath . . .

OLYMPICS TIMELINE

776 BC Earliest mention of the Olympic Games. Cook Coroebus is first known winner.

462 BC The Games expand to become a five-day event.

388 BC 'Zane' statues introduced to shame cheating athletes.

AD 67 Nero glories in fake triumphs at Olympia.

393 Christian emperor Theodosius the Great bans the Olympic Games.

426 Theodosius II orders the demolition of the temple of Zeus.

580 Earthquake destroys Olympia.

1612 Robert Dover launches his Olimpick Games at Chipping Campden in England.

1796–1798 An 'Olympic Festival' in Revolutionary France introduces the metric system to sport.

1829 First archaeological excavation of ancient Olympia.

1850 William Penny Brookes founds Much Wenlock Olympian Games in England.

1892 Baron Pierre de Coubertin creates the

International Olympic Committee (IOC).

1896 The inaugural modern Olympic Games are held in Greece. James Connolly is the first champion in 1,527 years and Spiridon Louis wins the marathon.

1900 Paris Olympics, integrated with World's Fair and lasting for months.

1904 St Louis Olympics, again integrated with World's Fair and including events for schoolboys and Irish Americans.

1906 The 'intercalated' Games in Athens, now regarded by the IOC as unofficial.

1908 London Olympics. Athletes parade with their national flags. Dorando Pietri collapses in the marathon.

1912 Stockholm Olympics. Jim Thorpe wins the pentathlon and decathlon. First marathon death. International Amateur Athletics Federation founded to fix the rules.

1913 Thorpe stripped of his medals for 'professionalism'. (Restored in 1982).

1916 Games cancelled: 1st World War.

1920 Antwerp Olympics. First appearance of the Olympic Flag and the Olympic Oath.

1924 Paris Olympics. First Winter Olympics at Chamonix.

1928 Amsterdam Olympics. Women first

appear in gymnastics and track & field events. Afterwards banned (until 1960) from running events longer than 200 m. First appearance of the Olympic Torch.

1932 Los Angeles Olympics.

1936 Berlin Olympics. Hitler uses Games for propaganda. Jesse Owens wins four golds. First torch relay from Greece.

1940, 1944 Games cancelled: 2nd World War.

1948 London Olympics. Forerunner of Paralympic Games at Stoke Mandeville.

1952 Helsinki Olympics.

1956 Melbourne Olympics. First political boycotts.

1960 Rome Olympics. Cyclist dies.

1964 Tokyo Olympics. South Africa banned because of its apartheid policy (until 1992).

1968 Mexico City Olympics. Black Power protest. First gender testing. Beginning of Special Olympics.

1972 Munich Olympics. Terrorists kill 11 Israeli athletes. First full-scale drugs testing.

1976 Montreal Olympics. Boycott by 30 African nations.

1980 Moscow Olympics. Boycott by more than 60 countries.

1984 Los Angeles Olympics. Boycott by

Eastern Bloc countries. First women's marathon leads to 'Scheiss rule'.
1988 Seoul Olympics. First professionals admitted. Ben Johnson tests positive for drugs.
1992 Barcelona Olympics.
1996 Atlanta Olympics is the first to be organised without government support.
1998 Scandal revealed of IOC members taking bribes from would-be host cities.
2000 Sydney Olympics.
2004 Athens Olympics. City makes a loss.
2008 Beijing Olympics.
2012 London's third Olympic Games.
2016 Rio Olympics.

FINDING OUT MORE

Among the sources used for this book:

The Complete Book of the Olympics
    David Wallechinsky and Jaime Loucky, Aurum Press
The Olympics' Strangest Moments
    Geoff Tibballs, Robson Books
Olympic Museum, Lausanne, Switzerland

GLOSSARY

anabolic steroids
Synthetic hormones
illegally used by some
athletes to increase their
muscle mass and strength.

boycott A decision not
to participate, usually for
political or moral reasons.

craps A gambling game
played with two dice.

grits In the southern
United States, a breakfast
dish of coarsely ground
and boiled hulled corn.

gymnasium In Ancient
Greece, a centre for both
physical training and
intellectual pursuits.

'hitting the wall'
Fatigue suffered by
marathon runners when
their glycogen levels run
low.

Hoplite A citizen-soldier
of one of the city states in
Ancient Greece.

masking agent A
compound taken by an
athlete to hide the
presence of illegal
substances in urine tests.

Olympiad A four-year
period which gives its
number to the Olympic
Games held within it.

ticker-tape parade A
celebration peculiar to the
centres of American cities,
in which masses of
shredded paper are fired
into the air to give a
snow-storm effect.

World's fair A large
public exhibition designed
to show off commercial,
scientific and artistic
achievements.

INDEX

OLYMPIC BESTS INDEX

A handy reference guide to the Olympic records scattered throughout the pages of this book: